Ohio State University
Columbus, Ohio

Written by Roland Becerra and Adam Jardy

Edited by Adam Burns, Matt Hamman, Kimberly Moore, and Jon Skindzier

Layout by Meghan Dowdell

Additional contributions by Omid Gohari, Christina Koshzow, Chris Mason, Joey Rahimi, and Luke Skurman

COLLEGE PROWLER®

ISBN # 1-4274-0107-1
ISSN # 151-0560
© Copyright 2006 College Prowler
All Rights Reserved
Printed in the U.S.A.
www.collegeprowler.com

Last updated 5/15/2006

Special Thanks To: Babs Carryer, Andy Hannah, LaunchCyte, Tim O'Brien, Bob Sehlinger, Thomas Emerson, Andrew Skurman, Barbara Skurman, Bert Mann, Dave Lehman, Daniel Fayock, Chris Babyak, The Donald H. Jones Center for Entrepreneurship, Terry Slease, Jerry McGinnis, Bill Ecenberger, Idie McGinty, Kyle Russell, Jacque Zaremba, Larry Winderbaum, Paul Kelly, Jon Reider, Team Evankovich, Lauren Varacalli, Abu Noaman, Jason Putorti, Mark Exler, Daniel Steinmeyer, Jared Cohon, Gabriela Oates, David Koegler, and Glen Meakem.

Bounce-Back Team: Alan Overholser, Mandy Heth, and Casey Clark.

College Prowler®
5001 Baum Blvd.
Suite 750
Pittsburgh, PA 15213

Phone: 1-800-290-2682
Fax: 1-800-772-4972
E-Mail: info@collegeprowler.com
Web Site: www.collegeprowler.com

College Prowler® is not sponsored by, affiliated with, or approved by Ohio State University in any way.

College Prowler® strives faithfully to record its sources. As the reader understands, opinions, impressions, and experiences are necessarily personal and unique. Accordingly, there are, and can be, no guarantees of future satisfaction extended to the reader.

© Copyright 2006 College Prowler. All rights reserved. No part of this work may be reproduced or transmitted in any form or by any means, including but not limited to, photocopy, recording, or any information storage and retrieval systems, without the express written permission of College Prowler®.

Welcome to College Prowler®

During the writing of College Prowler's guidebooks, we felt it was critical that our content was unbiased and unaffiliated with any college or university. We think it's important that our readers get honest information and a realistic impression of the student opinions on any campus—that's why if any aspect of a particular school is terrible, we (unlike a campus brochure) intend to publish it. While we do keep an eye out for the occasional extremist—the cheerleader or the cynic—we take pride in letting the students tell it like it is. We strive to create a book that's as representative as possible of each particular campus. Our books cover both the good and the bad, and whether the survey responses point to recurring trends or a variation in opinion, these sentiments are directly and proportionally expressed through our guides.

College Prowler guidebooks are in the hands of students throughout the entire process of their creation. Because you can't make student-written guides without the students, we have students at each campus who help write, randomly survey their peers, edit, layout, and perform accuracy checks on every book that we publish. From the very beginning, student writers gather the most up-to-date stats, facts, and inside information on their colleges. They fill each section with student quotes and summarize the findings in editorial reviews. In addition, each school receives a collection of letter grades (A through F) that reflect student opinion and help to represent contentment, prominence, or satisfaction for each of our 20 specific categories. Just as in grade school, the higher the mark the more content, more prominent, or more satisfied the students are with the particular category.

Once a book is written, additional students serve as editors and check for accuracy even more extensively. Our bounce-back team—a group of randomly selected students who have no involvement with the project—are asked to read over the material in order to help ensure that the book accurately expresses every aspect of the university and its students. This same process is applied to the 200-plus schools College Prowler currently covers. Each book is the result of endless student contributions, hundreds of pages of research and writing, and countless hours of hard work. All of this has led to the creation of a student information network that stretches across the nation to every school that we cover. It's no easy accomplishment, but it's the reason that our guides are such a great resource.

When reading our books and looking at our grades, keep in mind that every college is different and that the students who make up each school are not uniform—as a result, it is important to assess schools on a case-by-case basis. Because it's impossible to summarize an entire school with a single number or description, each book provides a dialogue, not a decision, that's made up of 20 different topics and hundreds of student quotes. In the end, we hope that this guide will serve as a valuable tool in your college selection process. Enjoy!

OMID GOHARI ○ CHRISTINA KOSHZOW ○ CHRIS MASON ○ JOEY RAHIMI ○ LUKE SKURMAN ○
The College Prowler Team

OHIO STATE UNIVERSITY
Table of Contents

By the Numbers............................ **1**

Academics **4**

Local Atmosphere **10**

Safety & Security **16**

Computers................................. **21**

Facilities..................................... **26**

Campus Dining.......................... **31**

Off-Campus Dining **38**

Campus Housing **47**

Off-Campus Housing................ **59**

Diversity..................................... **63**

Guys & Girls............................... **68**

Athletics..................................... **73**

Nightlife..................................... **80**

Greek Life **87**

Drug Scene................................ **92**

Campus Strictness **97**

Parking......................................**101**

Transportation **106**

Weather **110**

Report Card Summary **114**

Overall Experience **115**

The Inside Scoop.....................**119**

Finding a Job or Internship **124**

Alumni **126**

Student Organizations............**128**

The Best & Worst.....................**130**

Visiting......................................**132**

Words to Know........................**136**

Introduction from the Author

"What made you decide to come all the way over here?" is usually the first question I'm asked when I tell someone I'm from Texas. It's either that or: "Is everything really bigger in Texas?" . . . but that's a story suited for another time. Anyway, coming to Ohio State was largely due to luck. I hadn't applied to many colleges—only three, actually—but I decided to choose whichever was the farthest away from home, and, lo and behold, that happened to be the esteemed university in which I now reside. What a college prowler I was, huh?

I didn't know what to expect when I first arrived in Columbus, but as time went by, I realized that I had (luckily) chosen a school that suited my needs. For starters, not only is Ohio State a distinguished school, but it also perfectly blends an easygoing environment with a genuine emphasis on academics. It's also home to sports programs with a strong following, and its jam-packed football games and basketball hoopla really give you a sense of belonging to a community. Finally, being the largest city in Ohio doesn't hurt either. There are numerous things to do every single day of the week; so much so that it can be difficult to remember just why you're here—and that's to study, kids!

What you really want to know, though, is whether OSU is the right fit for you. You're curious to know if you're ready for what's coming. I'm sure everyone has a vague feeling of just what "college life" will be like, but from first-hand experience, let me tell you: feelings can be deceiving. Some people will find that it's not what they envisioned; it's not going to be a 24-hour party. So sit back, relax, and my co-author and I will try and inform you about the aspects of the University as best we can. Hopefully, you'll find that Ohio State has what you're looking for.

Roland Becerra, Author
Ohio State University

By the Numbers

General Information

Ohio State University
154 W 12th Ave.
Columbus, OH 43210

Control:
Public (non-profit)

Academic Calendar:
Quarter system

Religious Affiliation:
None

Founded:
1870

Web Site:
www.osu.edu

Main Phone:
(614) 292-OHIO

Admissions Phone:
(614) 292-3980

Student Body

Full-Time Undergraduates:
33,584

Part-Time Undergraduates:
3,925

Total Male Undergraduates:
19,736

Total Female Undergraduates:
17,773

Admissions

Overall Acceptance Rate:
76%

Total Applicants:
16,954

Total Acceptances:
12,822

Freshman Enrollment:
6,057

Yield (% of admitted students who actually enroll):
44%

Early Decision Available?
No

Early Action Available?
No

Regular Decision Deadline:
February 1

Must-Reply-By Date:
May 1

Applicants Placed on Waiting List:
288

Applicants Accepted from Waiting List:
88

Students Enrolled from Waiting List:
4

Transfer Applications Received:
3,654

Transfer Applications Accepted:
3,125

Transfer Students Enrolled:
1,807

Transfer Application Acceptance Rate:
85%

Common Application Accepted?
Yes

Admissions E-Mail:
askabuckeye@osu.edu

Admissions Web Site:
http://undergrad.osu.edu/admissions

SAT I or ACT Required?
Either

SAT I Range (25th–75th Percentile):
1070–1290

SAT I Verbal Range (25th–75th Percentile):
520–630

SAT I Math Range (25th–75th Percentile):
550–660

Top 10% of High School Class:
34%

Freshman Retention Rate:
87%

Application Fee:
$40

Financial Information

In-State Tuition:
$7,446

Out-of-State Tuition:
$18,033

Room and Board:
$7,275

Books and Supplies:
$1,080

Average Need-Based Financial Aid Package (including loans, work-study, grants, and other sources):
$9,149

Students Who Applied for Financial Aid:
65%

Students Who Received Aid:
52%

Financial Aid Forms Deadline:
February 1 for FASFA

Financial Aid Phone:
(614) 292-0300

Financial Aid E-Mail:
sfa-finaid@osu.edu

Financial Aid Web Site:
http://sfa.osu.edu

Academics

The Lowdown On...
Academics

Degrees Awarded:
Bachelor
Master
Doctorate
First Professional
Post-Certificate

Most Popular Majors:
5% Psychology
4% English Language and Literature
4% Communication Studies/ Speech Communication and Rhetoric
4% Family Resource Management Studies
4% Human Development and Family Studies

Undergraduate Schools:
College of the Arts
College of the Arts and Sciences
College of Biological Sciences
College of Dentistry
College of Engineering
College of Food, Agriculture, and Environmental Sciences
College of Human Ecology
College of Humanities
College of Mathematical and Physical Sciences
College of Medicine and Public Health

(Undergraduate Schools, continued)
Fisher College of Business
Michael E. Moritz College of Law
School of Communications
School of Environment and Natural Resources

Full-Time Faculty:
2,789

Faculty with Terminal Degree:
99%

Student-to-Faculty Ratio:
14:1

Average Course Load:
15 credit-hours/quarter

Graduation Rates:
Four-Year: 31%
Five-Year: 56%
Six-Year: 62%

Special Degree Options
Under advisement from a counselor, students can actually create their own personalized major. See your advisor for more details.

AP Test Score Requirements
Possible credit for scores of 3, 4, or 5.

IB Test Score Requirements
Possible credit and/or placement.

Did You Know?

The term "Buckeyes," in reference to Ohio State sports, actually comes from an older, broader use of the term—it used to refer to everyone who lived in the state of Ohio. The name was probably adopted because of the buckeye tree, the official tree of the state, or because Ohio is known as the "Buckeye State."

Don't watch your mailbox: **all grades and bills are sent electronically to your University account**, which can be accessed through OSU's network.

If you need some extra luck on finals, go to the main library and **rub the nose of former OSU president William Oxley Thompson**.

Best Places to Study:
Main Library, Mathematics and Statistics Learning Center, Starbucks, and the Oval during the spring quarter

Students Speak Out On...
Academics

"Professors are cool at OSU. Make sure you know your professors, and let them get to know you! Introduce yourself, and visit them during their office hours."

💬 "**Occasionally, you will have a foreign TA or professor**, but they are usually pretty easy to understand. All of my teachers have been eager to help, and most of them are very clever, inspiring characters."

💬 "**Teachers are pretty personable here**. You can e-mail them about something and get a reply within a few minutes."

💬 "The quality of the academics depends on the class. I've had some good teachers, and I've had some bad teachers. **History professors are really bad about mumbling and trailing off** when they are lecturing."

💬 "OSU professors are very nice. **If you miss class, it's not a big deal**, but don't make it a habit, because they do care about their students. The smaller classes take attendance at least once a week (without letting you know what day it will be) and count it as points towards (or against) your grade. College is completely different than high school, though; they won't call your parents if you don't come to class."

💬 "**Some classes are interesting**; it just depends on what you're interested in and how helpful the teacher is. Some professors are really interested in helping their students out."

Q "**Most of my teachers give good lectures and fair exams**, and they are always available and involved with their students. I've had a few, however, that are more interested in their research than teaching, and those ones aren't so great."

Q "**The teachers here are as diverse as the students.** Some are hard to understand and give the impression that they don't care if their students learn the information or not, while others make the material completely comprehensible and do everything in their power to make sure their students are learning what they need to learn."

Q "There are good professors, bad professors, ugly professors, and cute professors. **You'll either end up learning, falling asleep**, or, if you're anything like me, you'll be on the lookout trying to spot the hottest chick in the room."

Q "The teachers here are just as diverse as the student population; **they each bring something different to the picture**. Classes are interesting once you get into your major. The general education courses (GECs) here stink."

Q "Before you take any courses, I would advise you to **ask around and find out which professors are the ones to avoid**, which ones are pleasant, and which ones will probably end up being the cause of your nightmares for an entire three months."

Q "**The quality of professors depends on your major**. I am an English major, and most of my teachers are graduate students and are usually around my age group. I find them easier to contact and talk to than the professors."

Q "**The teachers at Ohio State vary**. Sometimes, you land great ones that really want to help students learn, but it's not that often."

The College Prowler Take On...
Academics

The feelings regarding professors and TAs are largely positive at OSU. Though feelings about the methods in which some courses are taught may differ a bit, one of the greatest advantages of OSU is the ease with which one can contact professors and TAs. OSU has a somewhat lax classroom environment compared to other schools, but don't be fooled: attending classes is still vital. Many courses weigh attendance and participation in your final grade, and beyond that, subject matter moves quickly and skipping even one class can put you in a deep hole. Don't make the mistake of thinking that a teacher will rigidly stick to the syllabus, either. Agendas change, and so do deadlines. You might be smart enough to skip a class for two weeks, but it won't matter if you miss a midterm because the date got changed and you didn't know.

School is what you make of it. OSU is a distinguished university with a top 25 national ranking, but that doesn't mean every professor will teach in a way that you prefer. It's a give-and-take situation. In some classes, there is a language barrier created by a foreign professor or TA; understanding calculus is difficult to begin with, but trying to learn from a teacher who speaks broken English makes it even harder. Luckily, most professors and TAs usually have at least one strong point that you can build from: constant communication. Talking to your instructors via phone, e-mail, or office visits can be incredibly important. Set up a meeting at a local coffee shop, or bake them a cake just to show them you mean business! Okay, so that might be going a bit overboard, but you get the idea.

B

The College Prowler® Grade on
Academics: B

A high Academics grade generally indicates that professors are knowledgeable, accessible, and genuinely interested in their students' welfare. Other determining factors include class size, how well professors communicate, and whether or not classes are engaging.

Local Atmosphere

The Lowdown On...
Local Atmosphere

Region:
Midwest

City, State:
Columbus, Ohio

Setting:
Largest city in Ohio

Distance from Cleveland:
2 hours, 20 minutes

Distance from Cincinnati:
1 hour, 45 minutes

Points of Interest:
The Book Loft of German Village
Brewery District
Columbus Zoo
German Village
Ohio Stadium
The Short North Historic Town
Wexner Center for the Arts

Closest Shopping Malls:
Columbus City Center
Easton Town Center
Lennox Shopping Center
Polaris

Closest Movie Theaters:
Arena Grand Theatre
175 W Nationwide
(614) 470-9900
www.arenagrand.com

Drexel Theatres
1247 Grandview Ave.
(614) 486-6114
www.drexel.net

Major Sports Teams:
Cincinnati Bengals (football)
Cincinnati Reds (baseball)
Cleveland Browns (football)
Cleveland Indians (baseball)
Columbus Blue Jackets (hockey)
Columbus Clippers (baseball)
Columbus Crew (soccer)

City Web Sites
http://columbusoh.about.com
www.columbuscene.com

Did You Know?
5 Fun Facts about Columbus:
- **The American Federation of Labor** was founded in Columbus.
- **Columbus is the state capital**, and it is Ohio's largest city.
- **David Harrison of Columbus owns the patent on the soft toilet seat**. Over one million are sold every year.
- Dave Thomas **opened the first Wendy's** in 1969 in Columbus.
- **The Columbus Clippers**, a AAA team, is a developing league for the New York Yankees.

Famous Columbians:
George Bellows, James "Buster" Douglas, Archie Griffin, Rutherford B. Hayes, Wayne "Woody" Hayes, Jack Nicklaus, James Thurber, and the music group Of A Revolution (OAR)

Local Slang:
That State up North – Michigan

Pop – The correct way to order a Coke or Pepsi

C-Bus – Abbreviation for Columbus

Students Speak Out On...
Local Atmosphere

> "Just about every major concert tour comes to Cleveland or Cincinnati. The Columbus Zoo is awesome! It's best to go when the weather is nice."

"Well, **Columbus is a major city** (the largest in Ohio), so there are lots of activities: fine arts, sports (professional hockey, soccer, and minor league baseball), and nightlife. There are also a couple of small colleges around, too, like Columbus State and Capital University."

"**You definitely want to visit Polaris and Easton Malls**. We have major theaters here, if you are into that, and there is a great fireworks display downtown for the Fourth of July. We also have the new arena district with tons of bars, restaurants, and a professional hockey team! Go Blue Jackets!"

"The atmosphere in Columbus is excellent. Especially during football season, **everyone is very supportive, friendly, and pepped up**. There are other universities around, but Ohio State is the most prominent. Downtown is easy to get to because of the buses. The Arena District and Short North provide lots of activities, as well."

"I live only five blocks off campus, and I love it. Not much to avoid around here; **just know that parties will run all the way to early morning**, so if you are a light sleeper, off-campus living might not be good for you."

"**OSU is a very chilled-out environment** with massive amounts of things to do every single day of the week—the problem is just waking up the next day for classes."

Q "**Columbus is the perfect little big city**. I'm sure there are other schools around, but who cares when you go to Ohio State? Stay out of dark alleys and Chittenden, and visit the Newport—it is the longest-running rock club in America!"

Q "**Take a trip downtown, just to visit**. You can even take a trip to a different city on the weekends—Cincinnati is about an hour and a half away from Columbus, Dayton is an hour away, and Cleveland is about two or three hours away."

Q "Every once in a while, **a few famous people might come to the clubs** or throw a concert. Other than that, you will have to go out and look for fun—just don't get in trouble doing it."

Q "Columbus is a great town; **there's always something to do**, or so I hear. I actually haven't had much of a reason to venture off campus, since virtually everything I need is right here. I've got access to Target and the movies by way of COTA, and that's all I really need."

Q "**There are five concert venues, three major shopping malls, and a lot of cool museums** such as the COSI Science Center and the Riffe Art Gallery downtown. There is an area of town called the Short North that has a lot of really funky art galleries, too. For a small, Midwestern city, it's pretty cultured and sophisticated."

The College Prowler Take On...
Local Atmosphere

Concerts, theatres, a zoo, malls, museums, and just about anything else can be found within the confines of Columbus. There are always numerous activities and events taking place, giving residents a variety of entertainment options to choose from. The Buckeye vibe permeates all of the surrounding area, and students see Columbus as a friendly town. Don't be fooled by the Midwest stigma of blandness or ignorance—most of the townies are glad to see you, and they will greet you with a smile. Columbus also sees a surprising number of cultural and entertainment events each year. With a wide variety of music scenes, numerous touring theater groups, and local sports teams, there is something for everyone to enjoy. The city is also very close—albeit, by vehicle—to cities such as Cleveland and Cincinnati, which provide even more activities. A weekend trip to one of these cities is not at all out of the question and will allow you to see concerts and sporting events you might have missed otherwise.

You cannot discuss the local atmosphere without discussing Buckeye sports. Foremost of these is football, obviously, and during football Saturdays, everyone watches the game—and we mean everyone. If you're looking to get shopping done, game day is the perfect time to do it. Be sure to get back in before the game ends, however, since roads in Columbus become massive parking lots as 105,000 people try to drive home afterward.

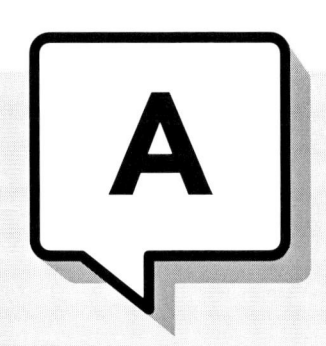

A

The College Prowler® Grade on
Local Atmosphere: A

A high Local Atmosphere grade indicates that the area surrounding campus is safe and scenic. Other factors include nearby attractions, proximity to other schools, and the town's attitude toward students.

Safety & Security

The Lowdown On...
Safety & Security

Number of OSU Police Officers:
56

Emergency Phone:
(330) 287-0111

Safety Services:
Escort Service: (614) 292-3322
RAD (Rape Agression Defense)
Ohio State Student Safety Service

Health Services:
Alcohol assistance
Basic medical services
Condom Club
HIV testing
OSU Anxiety and Stress Disorders Clinic
OSU Counseling and Consultation Services

Health Center Office Hours:
Monday–Friday
8 a.m.–4:30 p.m.

Did You Know?

The **OSU Escort Service provides safe transportation around and near campus** seven days a week, from early evening until 3:30 a.m.

The Student Health Center offers **free anonymous HIV testing** for all students.

Students Speak Out On...
Safety & Security

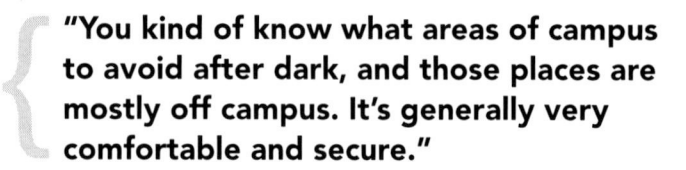

> "You kind of know what areas of campus to avoid after dark, and those places are mostly off campus. It's generally very comfortable and secure."

Q "Lately, the security hasn't been all that great on campus—but it's getting better. **There is a women-only transportation service offered at night**, which is helpful and is used frequently."

Q "OSU is really safe. We have an escort service that you can call 24/7. **You are also never out of sight of a blue-light call-box** that you can use to access the police, fire department, or an ambulance."

Q "**As a girl, it's scary to walk by yourself**. This is not because there are hoodlums everywhere, but because it is a rather large city, and bad things can happen."

Q "**They try really hard, I guess, but there could definitely be more cops around campus**, especially from a girl's point of view. I definitely don't feel like its safe enough to walk alone at night."

Q "**Everyone advises against walking around campus at night, or at least, against doing so alone**, but I've never had a problem with it. There have been nights when I didn't leave the library until 11 p.m., and I didn't feel nervous at all about walking back to my dorm—especially when there's at least one emergency blue-light visible from anywhere on campus."

Q "**I find campus to be extremely safe**; I have never had any problems with theft or vandalism at the dorms. Off campus is a little more hairy, but for a city as large as this, it's relatively safe. I have never once been scared to walk by myself anywhere on campus at all."

Q "In any place, you have to be careful, but the campus is pretty safe. **You just have to watch out off campus**, but nothing has happened to anyone I know. Plus, there are plenty of services available for rides."

Q "**Rapists and riots**: these two things alone should be reason enough to not feel safe, whether you are a man or a woman."

Q "I feel that the campus and its surrounding areas are very safe. **There are constantly police around (on bikes, horses, cars, and on foot)**, and there are several blue-lights (although I've never used one). I live off campus, and I don't walk alone by myself very often, but it's very safe to walk on campus at all hours."

Q "I have never felt unsafe at any point since I started at OSU. I have heard several stories about people's belongings getting stolen (**one of my friends had her stereo stolen out of her car**). Generally, as long as there are a lot of cars in the parking lot, then you have nothing to worry about."

Q "**Campus safety is rather good**—a lot of the troubles that come out of unfortunate situations are due to people either being or living in secluded areas. As for security, I haven't had any of my possessions stolen or tampered with in my dorm since I've been here."

Q "Let me just tell you that **bike cops rule**! No matter how hard you try, you just can't get away!"

The College Prowler Take On...
Safety & Security

As with many areas, the off-campus spots are those most prone to problems, and generally speaking, students report few problems on campus throughout the year. A great benefit to being an OSU student is the courtesy shuttle that takes students back to the residence halls. Another valuable tool is the blue-light call-box, which can be used to notify campus police in case of emergency. These call-boxes are scattered all over campus, and students say that security will respond quickly to such calls. Due to a number of reported rapes, and the massive lack of self-control (especially during Ohio State vs. Michigan State games), security has been increased around campus. OSU has gotten a bad rap from the media over the past few years, and with good reason—people overturning cars and burning furniture in the streets is a pretty big safety risk. While this behavior certainly isn't normal, it has occurred in the past. The biggest riot threat is in the spring, during an annual block party on Chittenden called "Chitfest," which now results in campus practically turning into a police state. If you don't want to run into law enforcement during these times, don't leave your house—period.

The bottom line regarding safety at OSU and Columbus is learning which areas to stay away from—especially during the night—and making intelligent decisions. Given its history, it's no surprise that OSU students are only beginning to feel really safe; hopefully, however, the University will continue to improve the current environment, and more secure feelings can take root.

B-

The College Prowler® Grade on
Safety & Security: B-

A high grade in Safety & Security means that students generally feel safe, campus police are visible, blue-light phones and escort services are readily available, and safety precautions are not overly necessary.

Computers

The Lowdown On...
Computers

High-Speed Network?
Yes

Wireless Network?
No

Number of Labs:
20

Number of Computers:
451 Windows, 816 Mac

Operating Systems:
Windows
Mac OS

Free Software

Acrobat Reader and Eudora

Discounted Software

Visit *http://oit.osu.edu/site_license* for a current list

24-Hour Lab

Baker Systems in the engineering building

Charge to Print?

10 cents per page, automatically deducted from your Buck-ID. $10 is deposited onto your Buck-ID every quarter for printing purposes only.

Did You Know?

Each student is issued an OSU e-mail address that is used throughout their college career. Upon graduation, students have the option of continuing to use the account.

For a **complete list of computer labs and operating hours**, check out *http://scc.osu.edu*.

Students Speak Out On...
Computers

> **"There are tons of computer labs on campus. There is at least one lab in every building, but some labs are busier than others."**

💬 "**Computer labs are not crowded** because everyone brings their own computer. If you do not bring your own, you will be hated by your roommates, because you will be using theirs often, whether you think you will or not."

💬 "Bring your own computer, it makes things much easier. I can usually find a computer when I need one on campus because there are so many computer labs. **The computer labs in the mechanical engineering and chemical engineering building are wonderful**; however, they are only open to students within those majors."

💬 "It is more convenient to bring your own computer, but the computers are very accessible. Some are even open 24/7. **The connection speed is very fast, and you can access anything you want**."

💬 "The computer network is fast. **It is truly amazing**! I think it is very good to have your own computer, just so you can use it for yourself whenever you're in your room, but most dorms have computer labs, and there are public computing sites everywhere on campus. It's pretty easy to get on a computer wherever you go. I brought my own computer with me last year to the dorm."

💬 "If you want your own computer, bring it. It just makes things easier. But **there are plenty of labs,** and they are never so crowded that you cannot get your work done."

Q "**The Younkin Success Center provides a good source of computers** that are usually running very well and are not that crowded. Libraries and things are usually much more crowded during finals, but otherwise, everything is usually available when you need it."

Q "**I found there to always be an open computer lab**, no matter where you are on campus. Many dorms even have a small lab in their building. It turned out that I wanted to write my papers in my pajamas at 3 a.m. in my room, so I brought my own computer."

Q "**Many of the professors have begun to use the Internet as a helpful guide for their courses,** so it is extremely important that you bring a computer which you can use at any time of the day. Baker Systems is open 24 hours a day, but it's a whole lot better to stay in your room and check your e-mail from there."

Q "The computer network is very fast. **You don't need a computer, but everyone brings their own**, and it's very helpful to have one since some classes are online. You also have to check your mail, grades, and schedule online—so save yourself the trouble and bring one."

Q "Definitely bring your computer! **A computer in the room is a must**. Anyone who's said that they got along fine using the computer labs their freshman year is lying to you. The bottom line is that you'll be way less stressed out if you've got your own computer—trust me."

Q "**Computer labs aren't always open when you need them**, and they can be a pain in the butt to get to. Buy your own, put it in your room, and use it whenever the hell you feel like it; it'll make your life much easier."

The College Prowler Take On...
Computers

At OSU, the computer has become extremely important as a tool for everyday use by the professors and the University itself. Information such as assignments, reminders, and class updates need to be accessed through the University's network, and teachers are increasingly relying on the Internet as a teaching tool. This makes easy access to a computer vital. The majority of students agree that getting your own computer is preferred; if that isn't possible, however, there are numerous labs around campus. Only one of these is open 24 hours, though, so access is somewhat limited.

Ideally, you should bring your own computer (and don't forget to buy an Ethernet cord!). There is nothing better than having the security of being able to work on papers or do online research in your own room. Not only that, but AOL Instant Messenger has a solid grip on social life at OSU, so be prepared to constantly update your profile and find new ways to say how much you hate homework! You'll want to check your e-mail often, too: OSU e-mails both grades and bills. While the computer labs are more than adequate to meet student needs (with only a few crowding problems, during the busiest times), having your own personal system is clearly the way to go.

B

The College Prowler® Grade on Computers: B

A high grade in Computers designates that computer labs are available, the computer network is easily accessible, and the campus' computing technology is up-to-date.

Facilities

The Lowdown On...
Facilities

Student Centers:
Drake Center
The Ohio Union

Athletic Centers:
Adventure Recreation Center (ARC)
Jesse Owens North and South
Recreation and Physical Activity Center (RPAC)

Campus Size:
3,411 acres

Libraries:
Beyond the William Oxley Thompson Library (also known as the Main Library), there are over 50 specialized libraries located across campus. For a complete list, check out: *www.lib.ohio-state.edu/libs*

Popular Places to Chill:
Cup O' Joe at the Lennox
Numbers Garden
Ohio Union
The Oval
Starbucks on High Street

What Is There to Do on Campus?

In the evenings, there are many activities to choose from, such as student readings, open-mic nights, and plays. If you are between classes and have a couple of hours to spare, go to the Ohio Union and watch a bit of TV with fellow students. The Numbers Garden by Central Classroom is a fun place to relax and study. Along with these options, always watch for free entertainment on the Oval—provided by random protest groups or by Brother Jed.

Movie Theater on Campus?

No

Bowling on Campus?

No

Bar on Campus?

Yes, Buffalo Wild Wings, Larry's bar, the Out 'R Inn, and Woody's Place in the Ohio Union.

Coffeehouse on Campus?

Yes, Cup O' Joe in Lennox Center, Starbucks in the bookstore, Barnes & Noble, Brennen's across from campus, Café Aporpos, Café Corner on 3rd Avenue, and Caribou Coffee on Grandview.

Students Speak Out On...
Facilities

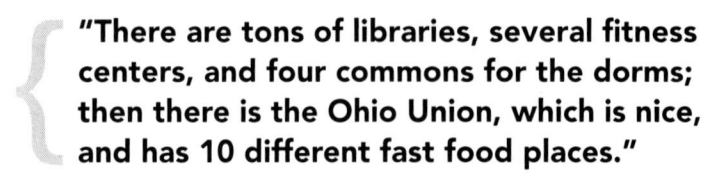

> "There are tons of libraries, several fitness centers, and four commons for the dorms; then there is the Ohio Union, which is nice, and has 10 different fast food places."

Q "**OSU facilities are awesome**—especially our athletic centers! Also, there are plenty of computer labs. As one of the biggest universities in the country, it definitely has all of the resources you need."

Q "The athletic center is awesome. The computer labs are good, too. The Ohio and Drake Unions are the student centers—**the Ohio Union even has a bar**!"

Q "Everything is maintained pretty well by the University. **The athletic centers are always getting in new equipment**, but they are usually very crowded during peak hours (3–6 p.m.)."

Q "Ohio State facilities are great! The gyms are really nice, as is the library. We have **amazing facilities** and a gorgeous campus."

Q "Everything you need is on campus. **You'll never have to go off campus** to get anything."

Q "**There is constant construction on campus**! Larkins is really improved since I got here! It used to be atrocious. Other than that, there's not a whole lot to complain about."

Q "Being an OSU athlete, I see the facilities offered to us and regular students. Larkins has been renovated, which was greatly needed. But overall, the facilities are abundant, and **most places are not that crowded**."

Q "Larkins, Jesse Owens, Main Library, and the Ohio Union—all of these are **excellent places to nourish the mind, body, and soul**."

Q "Nothing to complain about with regard to the facilities here in OSU—**there is always construction going on to improve the outlook of the campus**."

Q "**The Union is a great place for students to hang out**, whether you plan on grabbing a bite to eat at one of the many fast food places, or you just want to chill in one of the comfy lounge chairs upstairs."

Q "**There are awesome places to work out in**. I didn't know if there would be too much of an emphasis on having a good fitness center, and running around just doesn't do it for me. You should visit Larkins."

Q "Being in South Campus and having the Jesse Owens centers around is great. They even have a little concrete hockey floor to mess around in. There are also some basketball courts that are out in the open nearby, as well. **Some people who don't attend the University hang out there**, but it's not a big deal."

Q "The facilities are nice, although **they're not always kept as up-to-date as you think they would be** for the amount you are paying per quarter."

The College Prowler Take On...
Facilities

OSU provides its students with facilities to meet both mental and physical needs. Food courts can be found throughout campus, though the Ohio Union is the favored rest area between classes. In addition to the Main Library, which is due for renovations, there are a lot of smaller specialized libraries and reading rooms for almost every type of interest. Many students say that you don't actually have to leave campus to have everything you need.

If you're trying to get in shape after that figure-destroying weekend of keg parties, or if you just like to work out regularly, you're in luck—numerous fitness centers around campus are available to students. The facilities get a little crowded during peak workout times, but you can still get around them without too much hassle. Larkins has recently been renovated, and at over 45,000 square feet, it is one of the finest recreation centers in America. Jesse Owens North and South and other recreation facilities on campus are slightly more modern, but they are much smaller.

B+

The College Prowler® Grade on
Facilities: B+

A high Facilities grade indicates that the campus is aesthetically pleasing and well-maintained, facilities are state-of-the-art, and libraries are exceptional. Other determining factors include the quality of both athletic and student centers and an abundance of things to do on campus.

Campus Dining

The Lowdown On...
Campus Dining

Freshman Meal Plan Requirement?
Yes

Meal Plan Average Cost:
$3,650

Places to Grab a Bite with Your Meal Plan:

Buckeye Express North and South
Food: Salad bar, deli, grab 'n go
Location: North: 157 Curl Dr. South: Baker Hall East
Hours: Monday–Friday 7 a.m.–10 p.m.

Burrito Noches Café
Food: Mexican

Location: North Commons

Hours: Monday–Friday
9 p.m.–2 a.m.,
Saturday–Sunday
6 p.m.–2 a.m.

Campus Grind
Food: Sushi, sandwiches, salads, breakfast menu, and Starbucks coffee drinks

Location: Drinko Hall, McPherson Lab, and Vet Med

Hours: Drinko Hall: Monday–Friday 7:30 a.m.–2:30 p.m.; McPherson Lab: Monday–Thursday 7:30 a.m.–6 p.m., Friday 7:30 a.m.–4:30 p.m., Vet Med: Monday–Friday 7:30 a.m.–2 p.m.

Courtside Café and Grab 'n Go
Food: Salads, sandwiches, and entrees such as grilled chicken over jasmine rice, or pizza rustica

Location: RPAC

Hours: Monday–Sunday
10 a.m.–10 p.m.

The Deli
Food: Paninis, wraps

Location: The MarketPlace

Hours: Monday–Friday
10 a.m.–10 p.m.,
Saturday–Sunday
11 a.m.–8 p.m.

East/West
Food: Stir-fry and pasta dishes

Location: The MarketPlace

Hours: Monday–Friday
10 a.m.–9:45 p.m.,
Saturday–Sunday
11 a.m.–8 p.m.

Juice 2
Food: Smoothies, juices, vitamin supplements, and Seattle's Best coffee drinks

Location: RPAC

Hours: Monday–Friday
6 a.m.–1 a.m.,
Saturday 8 a.m.–1 a.m.,
Sunday 10 a.m.–1 a.m.

Kennedy Commons
Food: All-you-can-eat buffet

Location: 251 W. 12th Ave.

Hours: Monday–Friday
7:30 a.m.–10 a.m., 11 a.m.–2:30 p.m., 4:30 p.m.–8 p.m.,
Saturday 10 a.m.–2:30 p.m.,
4 p.m.–6:30 p.m.,
Sunday 10 a.m.–2:30 p.m.,
4 p.m.–7:30 p.m.

Mirror Lake Café
Food: Pizza, wings, subs, salads, soups, and smoothies

Location: 1760 Neil Ave.

Hours: Monday–Friday
7 a.m.–2 a.m.,
Saturday–Sunday
2:30 p.m.–2 a.m.

Morrill Commons
Food: All-you-can-eat buffet
Location: Morrill Tower
Hours: Monday–Friday
11 a.m.–2:30 p.m.,
4:30 p.m.–8 p.m.,
Saturday 10 a.m.–2:30 p.m.,
4 p.m.–6:30 p.m.,
Sunday 10 a.m.–2:30 p.m.,
4 p.m.–7:30 p.m.

Morrill Market
Food: Sandwiches, burgers, burritos and side dishes
Location: 1900 Cannon Dr.
Hours: Monday–Friday
7 a.m.–10 p.m.

North Commons
Food: All-you-can-eat buffet
Location: 157 Curl Dr.
Hours: Monday–Friday
11 a.m.–2:30 p.m.,
4:30 p.m.–8 p.m.,
Saturday 10 a.m.–2:30 p.m.,
4 p.m.–6:30 p.m.,
Sunday 10 a.m.–2:30 p.m.,
4 p.m.–7:30 p.m.

Oxley's By the Numbers
Food: Sandwiches, pizza, salad
Location: 2035 Millikin Rd.
Hours: Monday–Thursday
7 a.m.–7:30 p.m.,
Friday 7 a.m.–5 p.m.

The PAD
Food: Pizza, wings, sandwiches, sushi, and breakfast items
Location: The Drake Union
Hours: Monday–Friday
8 a.m.–1 a.m.,
Saturday–Sunday
4 p.m.–1 a.m.,
Delivery available daily from 5 p.m.–1 a.m.

Soup Spot and Fresh Greens
Food: Sandwiches and soups
Location: The MarketPlace
Hours: Monday–Friday
10 a.m.–10 p.m.,
Saturday–Sunday
11 a.m.–8 a.m.

Sprouts Café
Food: Vegetarian and vegan
Location: Kennedy Commons
Hours: Monday–Friday
11 a.m.–2:30 p.m.,
4:30 p.m.–8 p.m.,
Saturday 10 a.m.–2:30 p.m.,
4:30 p.m.–6:30 p.m.,
Sunday 10 a.m.–2:30 p.m.,
4:30 p.m.–7:30 p.m.

Stone Hearth
Food: Baked focaccias, breadsticks, and baked casseroles
Location: The MarketPlace
Hours: Monday–Friday
10 a.m.–10 p.m.,
Saturday–Sunday
11 a.m.–8 p.m.

StreetSweets

Food: Coffee and espresso drinks, smoothies, and pastries

Location: The MarketPlace

Hours: Monday–Saturday 7 a.m.–2 a.m., Sunday 10 a.m.–2 a.m.

ViewPoint Bistro

Food: Breakfast, salads, soups, appetizers, wraps and sandwiches, entrees, and Starbucks coffee drinks

Location: The Drake Union

Hours: Monday–Friday 11 a.m.–2 p.m., Tuesday–Thursday 4:30 p.m.–7 p.m.

24-Hour On-Campus Eating?

No

Other Options:

There is a Kosher deli as part of Douglass Dining Center or Uncle Dicky's parks on the fraternity quad on the weekends, with the popular favorite cheese fries and other heart-healthy foods.

Student Favorites:

Mirror Lake Café

Off-Campus Places to Use Your Meal Plan:

Check out *https://buckid.osu.edu/merchants/list.asp*

Sample restaurants include:

Adriaticos Pizza
Aladdin's Eatery
Apollo's
Boss Doggs
Brenen's Cafe
Buckeye Donuts
BW3s
Café Carmen
Charley's Steakary
Chipotle Mexican Grill
Cluck-U-Chicken
Cold Stone Creamery
Columbus Paninis
Domino's Pizza
Don Pablo's
Donato's Pizza
Flying Pizza
Gumby's Pizza
H.D. Dawg at the Ohio Union
Hound Dog Pizza
Indian Kitchen
Java Master
Jimmy John's
Johnny Rockets
Mad Mex
Mark Pi's Express
Melvin's Brick Oven
Minuteman Pizza
Mirror Lake Café
Moe's Southwest Grill
Morrill Commons
Morrill Market
Nick's Diner
Panera Bread
Papa John's Pizza
Pita Pit
Potbelly Sandwich Works
Quizno's Subs
Starbucks
Steak Escape Ohio Union
Steak 'n Shake
Subway
The Blackwell
The Cellar
The Taco Ninja
The Waiting Room Espresso Lounge
TJ's Restaurant
Ugly Tuna Saloona
United Dairy Farmers
Viewpoint Bistro
WG Grinders
Wendy's
Woody's Place

Students Speak Out On...
Campus Dining

> "Dining hall food isn't terrible—you just have to be discriminating in what you choose. Avoid the meat!"

Q "The food here is pretty good. The commons, Mirror Lake Café, Oxley's By the Numbers, and Buckeye Express all take meal plans. **There is also the Ohio Union, which has a food court**."

Q "I personally like Mirror Lake. **They don't have much of a variety**, but I like their subs."

Q "I'll be honest, the food is bad; in fact, **many people lose the Freshman 15 rather than gain it**. Mirror Lake Café is the best bet for using your meal plan here. Oxley's is another decent place to go. Normal dining commons are awful, though, and the Buckeye Express gets old after a few weeks (takeout food, mostly pre-packaged goods)."

Q "**There are tons of little places all over** that you can eat at, and some even let you use your Buck-ID (you can put money on it)."

Q "I basically eat at **Mirror Lake and Oxley's By the Numbers**. I despise the Commons."

Q "United Dairy Farmers (UDF) is a **cross between 7-11 and Baskin Robbins, and it is open 24 hours**. If you visit UDF at any given time, day or night, you're going to find students hanging around or making a quick stop. If you find yourself awake at 3 a.m. and you get a random craving for a sundae, UDF is where it's at."

The College Prowler Take On...
Campus Dining

Opinions vary regarding the food in the commons, but most are negative. Many students feel they are being ripped off when it comes to how much money they spend for their food. Mirror Lake is undoubtedly the most sought-after place to use your meal plan. Buckeye Express is also a student favorite, but fast food wears on you after a few months. The Ohio Union—again, fast food—also remains a viable option for those who are tired of the University's dining commons and crave something different, even if it's just for a day.

OSU dining needs help, and fast. If you've seen what some universities offer their students, you'll be really disappointed by Ohio's cafeteria food. The lack of variety means that everything gets old extremely fast. Mirror Lake is good, but you simply can't eat subs every day for every meal. The lines stretch outside the door at the beginning of the year, too, though they do eventually get shorter. You and your friends will also find yourselves coming up with totally unoriginal nicknames for Buckeye Express, as well. The one redeeming part of OSU's dining halls is that the staff is very nice. Too bad this doesn't translate into better-quality food.

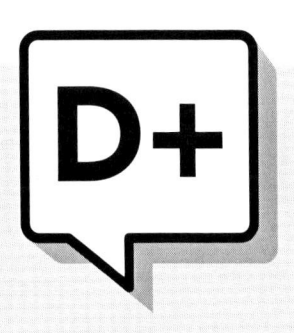

D+

The College Prowler® Grade on

Our grade on Campus Dining addresses the quality of both school-owned dining halls and independent on-campus restaurants, as well as the price, availability, and variety of food.

Off-Campus Dining

The Lowdown On...
Off-Campus Dining

Restaurant Prowler: Popular Places to Eat!

Adriatico's New York Style
Food: Pizza
265 W. 11th Ave.
(614) 421-2300
Cool Features: Closest to NY style pizza in Ohio.
Price: $5–$10 per person
Hours: Monday–Thursday
1 p.m.–1:30 a.m.,
Friday–Saturday
1 p.m.–2:30 a.m.,
Sunday 12 p.m.–12:30 a.m.

Alana's
Food: American bistro
2333 N. High St.
(614) 294-6783
Cool Features: Owned by Emeril's protegé, Alana Shock. Includes a fusion-style menu for meat lovers and vegetarians alike.
Price: $15–$25 per person
Hours: Tuesday–Thursday
5 p.m.–11 p.m.

Amazing Wok Chinese
Food: Chinese
1983 Henderson Rd.
(614) 451-1688
Cool Features: They have great daily lunch specials.
Price: $5–$10 per person
Hours: Daily 11 a.m.–11 p.m.

Apollo's Restaurant & Spirits
Food: Greek
1590 N. High St.
(614) 294-4006
Cool Features: Features music around the bonfire on selected nights.
Price: $5–$10 per person
Hours: Daily 11 a.m.–11 p.m.

BD's Mongolian Barbecue
Food: Oriental
6242 Sawmill Rd.
(614) 798-8300
www.bdsmongolian barbeque.com
Cool Features: Pick your own stir-fry ingredients; everything is cooked right in front of you.
Price: Lunch $7–$12, Dinner $12–$15
Hours: Sunday–Thursday
11 a.m.–10 p.m.,
Friday–Saturday
11 a.m.–11 p.m.

Blue Danube Restaurant
Food: Eclectic Mediterranean and American
2439 N. High St.
(614) 261-9308
Cool Features: Funky decor and great for a power lunch.
Price: $5–$10 per person
Hours: Sunday–Thursday
11 a.m.–2 a.m.,
Friday–Saturday
9 a.m.–2 a.m.

Blue Nile Ethiopian Restaurant
Food: Ethiopian
2361 N. High St.
(614) 421-2323
Cool Features: Daily lunch buffet. Uses traditional Ethiopian and Mexican spices.
Price: $10–$15 per person
Hours: Tuesday–Sunday
11:30 a.m.–2:30 p.m., and
5 p.m.–10 p.m.

Buca di Beppo
Food: Italian
343 N Front St.
(614) 621-3287
Cool Features: Family-style restaurant where you all share several dishes.
Price: $15–20 per person
Hours: Sunday–Thursday
11 a.m.–10 p.m.,
Friday–Saturday
11 a.m.–11 p.m.

Buckeye Donuts
Food: Donuts
1363 S. High St.
(614) 443-7470
Cool Features: Kind of place where everybody knows your name—no, really!
Price: $2–$6 per person
Hours: Daily 24 hours

Buckeye Hall of Fame & Café
Food: American
1421 Olentangy River Rd.
(614) 291-2233
Cool Features: Best sports bar in town. OSU memorabilia is everywhere on the walls.
Price: $7–$12 per person
Hours: Monday–Thursday
11 a.m.–11 p.m.,
Friday–Saturday
11 a.m.–12 a.m.,
Sunday 10 a.m.–10 p.m.

Buffalo Wild Wings
Food: Wings
515 S. High St.
(614) 221-4293
Cool Features: Big-screen TVs; good place to watch a game!
Price: $9–$15
Hours: Monday–Friday
11 a.m.–1:30 a.m.,
Saturday 11 a.m.–2:30 a.m.,
Sunday 11 a.m.–1 a.m.

Champps Americana
Food: American
1827 Olentangy River Road
(614) 298-0833
Cool Features: The portions are huge. Laid-back sports bar.
Price: $12–$18 per person
Hours: Monday–Friday
11 a.m.–1 a.m.,
Saturday–Sunday
11 a.m.–10 p.m.

The Cheesecake Factory
Food: American
3975 Townsfair Way
(614) 418-7600
Cool Features: Over 200 menu items, from Mexican to seafood.
Price: $15–$25 per person
Hours: Monday–Thursday
11 a.m.–11 p.m.,
Friday–Saturday
11 a.m.–12:30 a.m.,
Sunday 10 a.m.–10 p.m.

Chipotle Mexican Grill
Food: Mexican
1918 N. High St.
(614) 621-2601
Cool Features: What this place has that many Mexican places lack is their special spice!
Price: $8–$12 per person
Hours: Monday–Friday
11 a.m.–10 p.m.,
Saturday–Sunday
11 a.m.–8 p.m.

Cluck-U Chicken

Food: Chicken wings

2620 N. High St.

(614) 291-1010

Cool Features: Open late, great wings.

Price: $4–$8 per person

Hours: Monday–Saturday
4 p.m.–4 a.m.,
Sunday 4 p.m.–3 a.m.

Donato's Pizza

Food: Pizza

2084 N. High St.

(614) 294-5371

www.donatos.com

Cool Features: Owned by McDonald's.

Price: $8–$12 per person

Hours: Sunday–Thursday
11 a.m.–12 a.m.,
Friday–Saturday
11 a.m.–3 a.m.

Don Pablo's

Food: Mexican

1803 Olentangy River Rd.

(614) 291-6390

Cool Features: Big margaritas!

Price: $12–$20 per person

Hours: Sunday–Thursday
11 a.m.–10 p.m.,
Friday–Saturday
11 a.m.–11 p.m.

Dragonfly

Food: Vegetarian

247 King Ave.

(614) 298-9986

Cool Features: Nationally recognized vegetarian restaurant. Received the "Platinum Carrot" from the Aspen Center for Integrative Health.

Price: $15–$22 per person

Hours: Tuesday–Thursday
5 p.m.–10 p.m.,
Friday 5 p.m.–11 p.m.,
Sunday 11:30 a.m.–3 p.m.,
5 p.m.–11 p.m.

Flying Pizza

Food: Pizza

1812 N. High St.

(614) 294-1011

Cool Features: Best by-the-slice pizza shop around.

Price: $2–$8 per person

Hours: Sunday–Friday
10 a.m.–9 p.m.,
Saturday 10 a.m.–10 p.m.

Gumby's Pizza

Food: Pizza

2404 N. High St.

(614) 261-9800

Cool Features: Delivery is very quick. Try the pokey sticks!

Price: $8–$15 per person

Hours: Monday–Thursday
2 p.m.–3 a.m.,
Friday–Saturday
11 a.m.–3:30 a.m.
Sunday 11 a.m.–3 a.m.

Hounddogs Three Degree Pizza

Food: Italian

2657 N. High St.

(614) 261-4686

Cool Features: Two reasons for going to Hounddogs are that they are cheap and open 24 hours, but the greasy food will be what brings you back!

Price: $8–$12 per person

Hours: Daily 24 hours

Delivery hours: Weekdays 11 a.m.–2:30 a.m., Weekends 11 a.m.–3:30 a.m.

Jimmy John's

Food: Subs

1652 Neil Ave.

(614) 421-8800

Cool Features: Gourmet subs.

Price: $7–$10 per person

Hours: Daily 11 a.m.–8 p.m.

Mark Pi's Restaurant

Food: Chinese

171 E. Campus View Blvd.

(614) 781-2737

Cool Features: Daily specials. Can adjust spice level.

Price: $7–$12 per person

Hours: Monday–Thursday 11 a.m.–9:30 p.m., Saturday 12 p.m.–10 p.m., Sunday 4 p.m.–9 p.m.

Ming Flower Chinese Restaurant

Food: Chinese

475 Lazelle Rd.

(614) 885-8836

Cool Features: Take-out menu.

Price: $5–$10 per person

Hours: Monday–Thursday 11 a.m.–10 p.m., Friday–Saturday 11 a.m.–11 p.m., Sunday 11:30 a.m.–10 p.m.

The Pita Pit

Food: Pitas

1988 N. High St.

(614) 421-7482

Cool Features: You can head over to *pitapit.com* to check the nutritional information on your pita.

Price: $5–$8 per person

Hours: Sunday–Thursday 11 a.m.–3 p.m., Friday–Saturday 11 a.m.–4 p.m.

Steak N' Shake

Food: Burgers and fries

1918 N. High St.

(614) 297-7043

Cool Features: Has a drive-thru.

Price: $5–$9 per person

Hours: Open 24 hours

Subway
Food: Subs
515 S. High St.
(614) 461-7827
Cool Features: Fast food without it being fast food.
Price: $5–$8 per person
Hours: Monday–Friday
9 a.m.–9 p.m.,
Saturday–Sunday
9 a.m.–7 p.m.

Sunflower Chinese Restaurant
Food: Chinese
7370 Sawmill Rd.
(614) 764-7888
Cool Features: Owned by the brother of the owner of Ming Flower Restaurant.
Price: $5–$12 per person
Hours: Open daily
11:30 a.m.–11 p.m.

Tucci's
Food: Italian
35 N. High St.
(614) 792-3466
Cool Features: Charming bistro-style Italian restaurant with outdoor patio.
Price: $15–$25 per person
Hours: Monday–Thursday
5 p.m.–10 p.m.,
Friday–Saturday
5 p.m.–11 p.m.

Waffle House
Food: Breakfast
900 N. Wilson Rd.
(614) 272-9575
Cool Features: You can get breakfast anytime, but beware, it's often crowded during normal breakfast hours.
Price: $8–$12 per person
Hours: Daily 24 hours

Best Pizza:
Donato's

Best Chinese:
Amazing Wok Chinese

Best Breakfast:
Waffle House

Best Wings:
Buffalo Wild Wings

Best Place to Take Your Parents:
Buca Di Beppo

Closest Grocery Stores:
Kroger
1350 N High St.
(614) 294-2545

Giant Eagle
2801 N High St.
(614) 268-0976

Students Speak Out On...
Off-Campus Dining

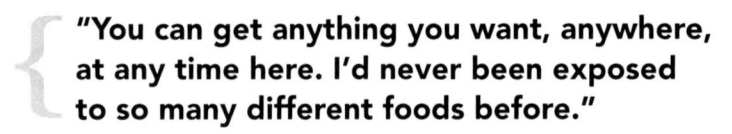

> "You can get anything you want, anywhere, at any time here. I'd never been exposed to so many different foods before."

Q "**I am going to get so fat here that it's not even funny**, there are so many wonderful restaurants and little delis to try out each and every day that it makes it impossible to lose weight."

Q "If Homer Simpson were a real person, I'm sure he would have no trouble finding something to satisfy his every need—and, yes, **we have a couple of donut shops around**!"

Q "**My waistline has gone to high heaven**. Truthfully though, there is a wide (no pun intended) variety of differing types of food that will, one way or another, satisfy even the choosiest people. I have gone on some romantic dates in some of the nicer places around town, and I have been to some low-down burger joints, which aren't all that bad when you have no other options around 4 a.m."

Q "As long as there's a local fast food restaurant around, I could care less if there are any other restaurants. Let me tell you, **double cheeseburgers for a dollar, it doesn't get any better than that**."

Q "Chipotle, Apollo's, and Mark Pi's—**need I say more**?"

Q "The restaurants off campus **make up for the average food on campus**."

Q "OSU is fabulous! **This is the reason Columbus is one of the five fattest cities in the U.S**. You name it, they have it: Italian, Korean, Chinese, Japanese, Mexican, Ethiopian, Indian, Pakistani . . . it's a smorgasbord of selections."

Q "Some nice restaurants are around, and **some `trendy' little eateries are all around campus**, as well. It's nice to chill out with all of my girls and just have a nice meal without having a guy around."

Q "**I like my food fast**. I stick by my guns when I say that if something takes longer to cook than it does to eat, then it has no place inside my stomach!"

The College Prowler Take On...
Off-Campus Dining

The verdict is overwhelmingly positive when it comes to dining in Columbus. There is such a wide selection of different types of food that it actually becomes very difficult to find something everyone can agree on (the exact opposite of the problem you'll run into while eating on campus). No matter what type of food you're looking for, you'll find it here. Prices don't seem to be a big issue for students, and everything is rather manageable, even for the cost-minded. Many restaurants also accept money from your Buck-ID card, making off-campus dining an even more attractive option.

There are so many places to choose from that just deciding where to get pizza can become an ordeal. Remember that many places around campus also deliver; tip the drivers well, though, because driving around campus is rough. A growing number of ethnic restaurants have sprung up throughout the city. Conveniently enough, most can be found along High Street, so you don't have to walk far. Most restaurants are open very late, but be sure to call ahead before you make the trip. The eateries around Columbus more than make up for the lack of dining options at OSU; eating out too much can get expensive, however, not to mention fattening—you'll probably want to make use of those athletic facilities after a few nights on the town. Try as many restaurants as you can, and by the end of your first semester, you'll already have a handful of favorites.

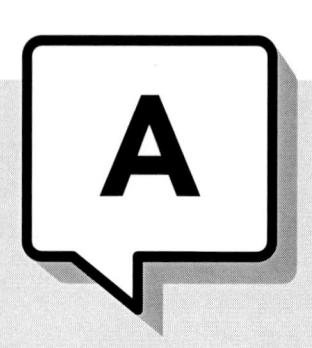

The College Prowler® Grade on
Off-Campus Dining: A

A high Off-Campus Dining grade implies that off-campus restaurants are affordable, accessible, and worth visiting. Other factors include the variety of cuisine and the availability of alternative options (vegetarian, vegan, Kosher, etc.).

Campus Housing

The Lowdown On...
Campus Housing

Room Types:
Singles, doubles, super doubles, quads, suites

Undergrads Living on Campus:
25%

Number of Dormitories:
24

Number of University-Owned Houses:
13

Best Dorms:
Canfield Hall
Lincoln Towers
Morrill Tower
Neilwood Gables
Siebert Hall

Worst Dorms:
Morrison Towers

Dormitories:

Baker Hall East and Baker Hall West
Location: South Campus
Floors: 4 + basement
Total Occupancy: 328 in East, 402 in West
Bathrooms: Corridor
Coed: Yes
Residents: Freshmen, sophomores, juniors, and seniors
Room Types: Singles, doubles, and triples
Special Features: Computer lab, Buckeye Express, bike room, Baker Hall East is part of the John Glenn Institute Living-Learning program, and Baker Hall West is part of the Visual and Performing Arts Living-Learning program.

Barrett House
Location: North Campus
Floors: 4 + basement
Total Occupancy: 181
Bathrooms: In-room
Coed: Yes
Residents: Freshmen, sophomores, juniors, and seniors
Room Types: Doubles, triples, quads, and super doubles
Special Features: Air-conditioning, cafeteria, laundry facilities, weight/rec room, Tomorrow's Teachers and Biological Sciences Scholars programs.

Blackburn House
Location: North Campus
Floors: 4 + basement
Total Occupancy: 174
Bathrooms: In-room
Coed: Yes
Residents: Upperclassmen
Room Types: Doubles, triples, quads, and super doubles
Special Features: Air-conditioning, bike room, laundry facilities, weight/rec room, home of MUNDO Living-Learning program.

Bradley-Paterson Halls
Location: South Campus
Floors: 4 + basement
Total Occupancy: 350 in Bradley, 357 in Paterson
Bathrooms: Corridor, with a few exceptions
Coed: Yes
Residents: Freshmen, sophomores, juniors, and seniors
Room Types: Singles, doubles, triples, and quads
Special Features: Weight/rec room, connected to Siebert via basement, Honors residence hall, laundry facilities.

Canfield Hall
Location: South Campus
Floors: 4 + basement
Total Occupancy: 312
Bathrooms: Corridor
Coed: Yes (though the 4th floor is female-only)

(Canfield Hall, continued)

Residents: Freshmen, sophomores, juniors, and seniors

Room Types: Singles, doubles, triples, and quads

Special Features: Nursing and Allied Medical Professions Living-Learning programs, laundry facilities.

Drackett Tower

Location: North Campus

Floors: 12

Total Occupancy: 472

Bathrooms: Room

Coed: Yes

Residents: Upperclassmen

Room Types: Singles, doubles, and quads

Special Features: Kitchen and laundry facilities, weight/rec room, air-conditioning.

Fechko House

Location: South Campus

Floors: 2

Total Occupancy: 17

Bathrooms: Corridor

Coed: No, all women

Residents: Upperclassmen

Room Types: Singles, doubles

Special Features: Part of Alumnae Scholarship Housing (ASH), works in collaboration with the Alumnae Housing Scholarship Board, two kitchens, TV lounge, laundry and dining room, study areas.

German House

Location: South Campus

Floors: 2

Total Occupancy: 9

Bathrooms: Corridor

Coed: Yes

Residents: Upperclassmen

Room Types: Singles, one double, and one triple

Special Features: Highlights German language and culture, public lounge and kitchen.

Halloran House

Location: North Campus

Floors: 4

Total Occupancy: 138

Bathrooms: Room

Coed: Yes, by floor

Residents: Upperclassmen

Room Types: Doubles, triples, quads, and super doubles

Special Features: Mount Leadership Society Living-Learning program, air-conditioning, laundry facilities.

Hanley House

Location: South Campus

Floors: 3

Total Occupancy: 17

Bathrooms: Corridor

Coed: Yes

Residents: Upperclassmen

Room Types: Singles, doubles, and one triple

(Hanley House, continued)

Special Features: Alumnae Scholarship Housing, house manager delegates chores, food manager delegates ordering food for the house, computer and TV lounge, kitchen, dining room, front porch with swing, central heating/air-conditioning, and finished basement.

Haverfield House

Location: North Campus
Floors: 4
Total Occupancy: 165
Bathrooms: Room
Coed: Yes
Residents: Upperclassmen
Room Types: Doubles, triples, quads, and super doubles
Special Features: Air-conditioning, laundry facilities.

Houck House

Location: North Campus
Floors: 4
Total Occupancy: 163
Bathrooms: Room
Coed: Yes
Residents: Upperclassmen
Room Types: Doubles, triples, quads, and super doubles
Special Features: Air-conditioning, kitchen and laundry facilities, Women in Engineering Living-Learning program.

Jones Graduate Tower

Location: North Campus
Floors: 13
Total Occupancy: 212
Bathrooms: Private
Coed: Yes
Residents: Grad students
Room Types: Singles
Special Features: Air-conditioning, wall-to-wall carpeting, private bathrooms, swimming pool, kitchen, laundry facilities.

Lincoln House

Location: West Campus
Floors: 23
Total Occupancy: 416
Bathrooms: Room
Coed: Yes
Residents: Freshmen, sophomores, juniors, and seniors
Room Types: Doubles, quads
Special Features: Air-conditioning, kitchen and laundry facilities, Honors Living-Learning program.

Mack Hall

Location: South Campus
Floors: 4
Total Occupancy: 417
Bathrooms: Corridor
Coed: Yes
Residents: Freshmen, sophomores, juniors, and seniors

(Mack Hall, continued)

Room Types: Singles, doubles, triples, and quads

Special Features: Stadium scholarship, weight/rec room, cafeteria dining hall, and convenience store.

Morrill Tower

Location: West Campus

Floors: 23

Total Occupancy: 1,117

Bathrooms: Room

Coed: Yes

Residents: Freshmen, sophomores, juniors, and seniors

Room Types: Doubles, quads

Special Features: Air-conditioning, kitchen and laundry facilities, African American and substance-free Living-Learning programs.

Morrison Tower

Location: South Campus

Floors: 10 + basement

Total Occupancy: 464

Bathrooms: Corridor

Coed: Yes

Residents: Freshmen, sophomores, juniors, and seniors

Room Types: Singles, doubles, and quads

Special Features: Air-conditioning, International House, Spanish Language and Culture Living-Learning program, kitchen, laundry

Neil Avenue

Location: South Campus

Floors: 5

Total Occupancy: 186

Bathrooms: Corridor

Coed: Yes

Residents: Freshmen, sophomores, juniors, and seniors

Room Types: Singles, doubles

Special Features: TV lounge, conference room, the MarketPlace is located on the first floor, laundry facilities, study areas, vending machines.

Neilwood Gables

Location: North Campus

Floors: 4

Total Occupancy: 112

Bathrooms: Room

Coed: Yes

Residents: Upperclassmen

Room Types: Doubles

Special Features: Range stove, upperclassman Living-Learning program, and laundry facilities.

Norton House

Location: North Campus

Floors: 4

Total Occupancy: 145

Coed: Yes

Residents: Upperclassmen

Bathrooms: Room

Room Types: Doubles, quads, and super doubles

(Norton House, continued)

Special Features: Food, Agriculture, Pre-Veterinary, and Natural Resources Living-Learning programs, air-conditioning, weight/rec room, and laundry facilities.

Nosker House

Location: North Campus

Floors: 4

Total Occupancy: 642

Coed: Yes

Residents: Upperclassmen

Bathrooms: Room

Room Types: Doubles, quads, and super doubles

Special Features: Ford Living-Learning program, air-conditioning, laundry and kitchen facilities.

Park Hall

Location: South Campus

Floors: 11

Total Occupancy: 381

Coed: Yes

Residents: Freshmen, sophomores, juniors, and seniors

Bathrooms: Corridor

Room Types: Singles, doubles, and triples

Special Features: First-year residence hall, laundry and kitchen facilities.

Pennsylvania Place

Location: South Campus

Floors: 3

Total Occupancy: 28

Coed: Yes

Residents: Upperclassmen

Bathrooms: Shared by suites

Room Types: Singles, doubles

Special Features: Lounge, public kitchen, central air-conditioning.

Pomerene House

Location: South Campus

Floors: 3

Total Occupancy: 18

Coed: Yes

Residents: Upperclassmen

Bathrooms: 4

Room Types: Singles, doubles, and one triple

Special Features: Part of Alumnae Scholarship Housing (ASH), house manager delegates chores, food manager delegates ordering food for the house, finished basement, computer/TV lounge, kitchen, dining room, central heating/air-conditioning.

Scholars East

Location: South Campus

Floors: 3

Total Occupancy: 46

Coed: Yes

Residents: Upperclassmen

Bathrooms: 1 per 4 students

(Scholars East, continued)

Room Types: Doubles (singles for RAs)

Special Features: Two TV lounges, two public kitchens, laundry in building.

Scholars West

Location: South Campus

Floors: 2

Total Occupancy: 50

Coed: Yes

Residents: Upperclassmen

Bathrooms: 1 per 4 students

Room Types: Doubles (singles for RAs)

Special Features: Two public kitchens, two TV lounges, laundry in house.

Scott Hall

Location: North Campus

Floors: 4

Total Occupancy: 113

Coed: Yes

Residents: Upperclassmen

Bathrooms: Room

Room Types: Doubles, quads, and super doubles

Special Features: Health Sciences Scholars program, computer lab, laundry facilities, and weight/rec room.

Siebert Hall

Location: South Campus

Floors: 10

Total Occupancy: 303

Coed: Yes

Residents: Freshmen, sophomores, juniors, and seniors

Bathrooms: Corridor

Room Types: Singles, doubles, and quads

Special Features: Laundry and kitchen facilities, honors Living-Learning program, study rooms.

Smith Hall

Location: South Campus

Floors: 11

Total Occupancy: 426

Coed: Yes

Residents: Freshmen

Bathrooms: Corridor

Room Types: Singles, doubles, and quads

Special Features: Kitchen and laundry facilities, substance-free Living-Learning program, first-year residence hall.

Steeb Hall

Location: South Campus

Floors: 11

Total Occupancy: 426

Coed: Yes

Residents: Freshmen

Bathrooms: Corridor

Room Types: Singles, doubles and quads

(Steeb Hall, continued)

Special Features: First-year residence hall, kitchen and laundry facilities, weight/rec room, Engineering Focus Community.

Stradley Hall

Location: South Campus

Floors: 11

Total Occupancy: 642

Coed: Yes

Residents: Freshmen

Bathrooms: Corridor

Room Types: Singles, doubles, triples, and quads

Special Features: Kitchen and laundry facilities, weight/rec room, first-year residence hall, Social and Behavioral Sciences Focus Community.

Taylor Tower

Location: North Campus

Floors: 12

Total Occupancy: 576

Coed: Yes

Residents: Freshmen, sophomores, juniors, and seniors

Bathrooms: Room

Room Types: Doubles, triples, and quads

Special Features: Kitchen and laundry facilities, huge lounge area.

Worthington Building

Location: South Campus

Floors: 5

Total Occupancy: 140

Coed: Yes

Residents: Freshmen, sophomores, juniors, and seniors

Bathrooms: Shared by suites

Room Types: Singles, doubles

Special Features: Public lounge, community kitchen, central air-conditioning, laundry in building, study areas.

Housing Offered:

Singles: 4%

Doubles: 62%

Triples/Quads: 26%

Apartments: 8%

Bed Type

Extra-long twin

What You Get

Each room comes with at least one MicroFridge, desks, chairs, beds, lamps, ResNet Internet access, cable TV access, dressers, free campus and local phone calls, in-room voicemail, and window coverings.

Cleaning Services?

Students are responsible for cleaning their own rooms. Housekeeping staff are responsible for cleaning the public areas (hallways, lounges), public restrooms, and bathrooms shared by clustered rooms. Students with bathroom facilities in their individual rooms or suites are responsible for cleaning their own bathrooms.

Also Available

In terms of living, there are quiet-study and substance-free floors, as well as a whole host of special-interest housing. Some include the Tiernan Project, which has a whole floor of a dorm and is dedicated to community service, ICLC (InterClass Living Center) a freshman mentor program, MIF (Music Interest Floor), CIF (Computer Interest Floor), CLC (Community Living Center) and ILC (International Living Center).

Did You Know?

All campus residents get **free cable TV**.

Ohio State has started its own **student-run television station, BUCK-iTV**, available on the campus network.

Students Speak Out On...
Campus Housing

> "I definitely recommend South Campus dorms. North Campus and the Towers are too far away from everything. There are always activities on South Campus, and you're closer to Greek life."

Q "**We have three areas of dorms, with three different reputations**. I got a different area than I wanted, but I ended up loving it!"

Q "If you go to OSU, **stay in the Towers** because the other dorms are nasty."

Q "The dorms I've experienced at **North are not so bad**. They can be really good for studying, as they tend to be quieter than South. Your dorm experience basically depends on your roommates and/or floormates."

Q "I'm an RA at one of the North Campus dorms, and it's quiet. **South is a little more rowdy**."

Q "All I can say is this: **bring your own toilet paper**, or you will pay the price every time you sit down."

Q "**You definitely need to live in the dorms your freshman year**. The dorms are really friendly; everyone normally leaves their doors open, and it's a great way for you to meet new friends. South Campus most definitely is the place to be."

- "**Dorm life is okay for no more than two years**. Choose your roommate carefully! North dorms are for grade-minded, studious people who like things quiet. South is for people who like things loud. No clue about West; it's a long walk, though."

- "**North Campus dorms suck**. Most honor students live there, and it's really quiet. I lived there last year, and it was horrible!"

- "The dorms are okay. **The rooms are kind of small**, and floor bathrooms can get really sloppy. The North Campus dorms and the two Towers are better, for the most part, and have air-conditioning, but they kind of suck because those parts of campus are quiet and boring."

- "**Siebert Hall in South Campus was great**. I enjoyed the people that worked there and lived there. They are not too small, and they offer a plethora of opportunities."

- "**South Campus is fun, and it's easy to meet people**. I find the surroundings to be somewhat of a distraction when I'm trying to study. I would still live in South, though; you need to have fun in college."

- "**Home is where the heart is—every single dorm sucks**. I don't care if it's in South Campus, North Campus, or the Towers. They are all crappy."

The College Prowler Take On...
Campus Housing

There are three main housing quarters on campus: North, South, and the Towers. North Campus is considered the place for quiet living and for those who don't seek out a huge social life. South Campus dorms are a bit louder, since they house the majority of the incoming freshman class. Towers are nearly ignored because of their distance from the main campus. Most students agree that all the dorms could use some work—don't expect to be wowed by your living facilities.

The best advice is to choose an area to live in based on what type of environment you're most likely to enjoy. It really boils down to what attitude you have and what types of people you want to be around. North and the Towers tend to be less noisy and better places to study, overall. In these dorms, you get two rooms and your own bathroom, as well as air-conditioning. South Campus dorms are known throughout the University for a much more relaxed and outgoing atmosphere. Most South dorms do not have their own bathrooms, and they are generally smaller and uglier than North; you do have fewer people in each room, however. Another important thing to consider is location: most classes are held closer to North Campus, and this can mean a lot when it's below freezing outside and there's snow on the ground. All of the dorms are in sore need of updating—everything was built in the '50s and '60s, and you can tell—with the possible exception of the Towers. A final word of advice: if you have the chance, loft your bed and drop your desk. You'll see why.

C+

The College Prowler® Grade on
Campus Housing: C+

A high Campus Housing grade indicates that dorms are clean, well-maintained, and spacious. Other determining factors include variety of dorms, proximity to classes, and social atmosphere.

Off-Campus Housing

The Lowdown On...
Off-Campus Housing

Undergrads in Off-Campus Housing:
75%

Average Rent For:
Studio Apt.: $350–$390 per month
1BR Apt.: $400–$500 per month
2BR Apt.: $450–$600 per month

Popular Areas:
Lane, Norwich

For Assistance Contact:
Community Housing Services
www.osuoffcampus.com
(614) 292-0100

For rankings and input on realtors: pick up a copy of the OSU Renting Guide from Student Government or Off-Campus Student Services in the Ohio Union.

Students Speak Out On...
Off-Campus Housing

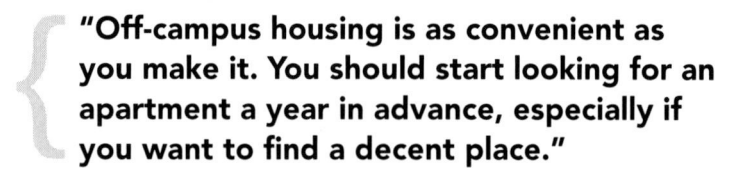

> **"Off-campus housing is as convenient as you make it. You should start looking for an apartment a year in advance, especially if you want to find a decent place."**

Q "There are nice apartments and houses off campus. Off-campus rent ranges anywhere from **$350–$550 a month, usually not including utilities**."

Q "**Don't move off campus until your sophomore year** or the end of your freshman year. The experience of living on campus is a lifetime memory—but it is definitely cheaper to live in off-campus housing."

Q "Usually, the **farther you go from campus, the cheaper and better it gets**."

Q "I love living off campus. I wish I would have moved out after my first year. Be prepared to be **responsible for a lot of bills and maintenance, though**."

Q "**Housing off campus is usually cheaper** than living on campus, if you do it right; although, there are plenty of sleazy rental companies that will try to get as much money out of you as possible."

Q "The housing off campus is okay. **It's kind of hard to find places right by campus**, but if you are willing to ride the bus or drive, then you are sure to find a great place to live."

Q "I live off campus, and **it's pretty convenient**. You really don't need a car, unless you want to go somewhere on the weekend, or unless you're lazy and drive to class."

Q "**Living off campus is a blast**, and it is definitely worth it! It's nice to have your own room and your own place yet still hang out with roommates."

Q "If you get looking early, you can find some decent housing. **It's comparatively cheaper than the dorms**, and you share a bathroom with fewer people. If you end up six blocks from campus, it's not worth it."

Q "There are **a lot of apartments and houses mostly east of campus**, some of which actually cost less than living in the dorms (if you get the right deal). First-year students have to live in the dorms, though."

Q "Pick your roommates and the house or apartment you want to live in early—both get **snatched up fast**. Everything is really close to campus, and many places are pretty much across the street!"

The College Prowler Take On...
Off-Campus Housing

Off-campus housing is highly recommended at OSU, but only after at least one year of campus life. It's almost expected that you'll move off campus eventually—the biggest question is when. Having your own place shouldn't cost any more than living in the dorms, and if you do it right, you can actually be paying less. Prices vary drastically depending on what you want, however. Planning early is the best idea, no matter what type of housing you seek—start looking after winter break, at the very latest. Pick roommates early (if applicable), and start looking at what's available. Wait too long, and you'll find yourself out of options and facing another year in the dorms. After you're done with freshman year in the residence halls, you have a better idea what campus life is like. Students recommend getting a quad with your best friends on South Campus as an alternative to moving into an apartment—at least for the second year. If you do move off campus quickly, try to live somewhere close. The number of people you meet plummets when you move out of the residence halls, so try to make as many friends as possible while you're in the dorms; you might be glad to have those connections later on.

Be sure that you're ready to pay your own bills, buy your own food, deal with neighbors (sans RA), and handle many other responsibilities before you decide to get your own place. If in doubt, check out the off-campus housing Web site and pick up a copy of the OSU renting guide. Most realtors in the area are also friendly, and they're quick to help students find housing and work through whatever problems may arise.

A-

The College Prowler® Grade on
Off-Campus Housing: A-

A high grade in Off-Campus Housing indicates that apartments are of high quality, close to campus, affordable, and easy to secure.

Diversity

The Lowdown On...
Diversity

Native American:
1%

Asian American:
5%

African American:
8%

Hispanic:
2%

White:
81%

International:
3%

Out-of-State:
9%

Most Popular Religions

There are many different religious groups that are represented. Catholic, Protestant, Lutheran, Jewish, and Muslim beliefs are some of the more highly visible, though these are just a few of the total. Non-denominational Bible studies are commonplace on campus, and there is no official University religious affiliation. All official places of worship are off campus.

Political Activity

The campus definitely has a liberal leaning. When President George W. Bush gave the commencement speech at spring graduation in 2003, a group of students organized a protest. Every time the president would speak, they would turn their backs on him. Anti-war demonstrations are common, as well as peace rallies. A local newspaper, the *Sentinel*, is one of the few voices that speaks for conservatism.

Gay Pride

OSU has a number of gay/lesbian groups such as Fusion and Gay, Lesbian, Bisexual and Transgender Student Services (GLBTSS). Columbus is an extremely open community with a large amount of gay and lesbian individuals. In fact, it is considered one of the five most permissive gay communities in America.

Economic Status

Due to problems with the budget, the state of Ohio does not help much when it comes to paying for higher education. You will not find a lot of poor students at Ohio State, for the simple reason that they cannot afford it. Most students range from lower-middle-class to upper-class.

Minority Clubs

There are various clubs in which any type of student can join. There is the All-Ethiopian Students Association, Turkish Student Association, the Hispanic Organization of Texas Students (HOTS), and numerous others. The Hale Center on South Campus is the African American Cultural Center. Check the union for information on other active minority clubs.

Students Speak Out On...
Diversity

> "I think OSU is very diverse, and they are always trying to make it even more so. The Diversity Action Plan is a big deal here. The administration is trying to ensure that OSU is racially and ethnically balanced to reflect what society is actually like."

- "We've got **one of the most diverse campuses** of any school in the Midwest. Lots of international students, and people of all sorts come here."

- "**The campus is really diverse**. That's one thing that OSU prides itself on."

- "There are people of many different races and religions here, but **they comprise a negligible percentage of the student body**. Most people here are white, and as a consequence, we have a reputation for being a school full of ignorant rednecks. We do have those types of people, but then again, this is the second largest school in the country."

- "**It's really easy to stay within your own comfort zone and never reach out** to another culture. One of the advantages to OSU is its rich cultural mixture. It would be a shame to waste an experience like this."

- "**It's not New York City**, but even coming from a diverse high school, I was really surprised at just how many different groups (ethnic, religious, political) are represented on campus. For any interest or belief, there's a group on campus for it."

Q "This campus is **so diverse it makes me sick**."

Q "**There is no diversity whatsoever. It's so bland.** Everywhere I look, it's as white as can be. Don't get me wrong, I have white friends, but if we want to create an environment that will get us prepared for the 'real world,' shouldn't there be more people of color?"

Q "**It's about as good as we can expect** for being in the Midwest. I think there is a good number of people who each bring their own perspective on things."

Q "I've read in the paper that there are more minorities than people realize because **people tend to stay within their own ethnic groups**. I think that might be true."

Q "It's **not as diverse as I would have hoped**."

Q "There are **many nationalities and ethnicities represented here**. Coming from a very small, homogenous town, it's pretty neat to hear five different languages being spoken just on a walk to class."

Q "It is **fairly diverse racially and politically**. We definitely have an active conservative scene on campus, which can be incredibly annoying, regardless of what you consider yourself politically. I personally hate the anti-abortion fetus truck that drives around campus, and of course, Brother Jed."

The College Prowler Take On...
Diversity

OSU students voice mixed feelings regarding diversity issues. The main population of the University is still overwhelmingly white, and though there has been a visible effort on the part of the school to increase this, there has been no drastic change in the number of minorities enrolled. Still, many feel that the changes necessary for creating a more diverse school are in the process of being made. In addition, recent articles in the *Lantern* (the student newspaper) have shown that, while there may be a significant minority population at OSU, most students tend to stay within their own cultural boundaries—the phenomenon of self-segregation.

The biggest drawback to OSU's student climate is a lack of racial diversity. Considering the school's Midwestern location, there is still a respectable number of cultures represented; however, this doesn't change the fact that minority students may feel like fish out of water, at times, in OSU's largely homogenous community. The redeeming factor is that there are many cultural clubs and organizations in the University, so minority students have a chance to meet each other and take better advantage of OSU's programs.

The College Prowler® Grade on Diversity: C-

A high grade in Diversity indicates that ethnic minorities and international students have a notable presence on campus and that students of different economic backgrounds, religious beliefs, and sexual preferences are well-represented.

Guys & Girls

The Lowdown On...
Guys & Girls

Men Undergrads:
53%

Women Undergrads:
47%

Birth Control Available?

Yes, through Student Health Services. Be sure to ask about the Condom Club.

Hookups or Relationships?

Most women are already taken, but there is also a large group of girls who are only out to have fun and think nothing more of it. There are also plenty of single guys around, looking for everything from hookups to long-term relationships. There is no real trend toward either end of the spectrum.

Best Place to Meet Guys/Girls

Bars are great places to meet up with people and have a friendly chat. Believe it or not, the library is also a great place to hang out with romantic interests. If the weather is nice, there is no place better than the Oval. Don't be afraid to wander the halls of your dorm, either.

The best time to find that special person is during the springtime. The flowers are blooming, the sun is shining, the campus looks beautiful, and lots of skin is shown. Lots of people hook up in the spring, only to have the relationship fall apart during the long summer break. Keep your chin up, and take advantage of the warm weather when you come back for fall quarter. During spring quarter, date people who live on North Campus or in the Towers—they have air-conditioning!

Dress Code

Students dress in all kinds of styles. You have emo, preppy, conservative, punk, hip hop, and many others. The prevailing color, however, is red. Even the homeless people around campus wear Ohio State clothing. When it's cold, though, not many people worry about making a fashion statement. During the spring is when you see who has style and who does not.

Did You Know?

Top Three Places to Find Hotties:
1. Red Zone
2. Four Kegs
3. NYOHS

Top Five Places to Hook Up:
1. Main Library
2. Four Kegs
3. Red Zone
4. The Oval
5. Newport Music Hall

Students Speak Out On...
Guys & Girls

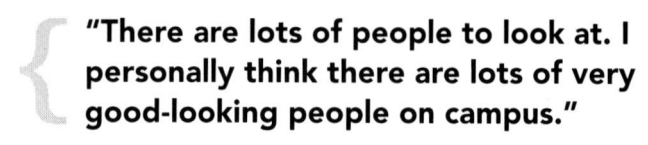

> **"There are lots of people to look at. I personally think there are lots of very good-looking people on campus."**

Q "I'm not checking out guys, but hey, I suppose they're hot. **Girls are hot**, too."

Q "I think that **there are more pretty girls than good-looking guys**, which kind of sucks, but that is only my opinion."

Q "I go here, so yes, the guys are hot, and from what I've seen in my two and a half years, **the female population is very attractive**."

Q "**The hot ones all hide until spring quarter**, actually. At least, that's when I notice them. Overall, I would say we're pretty much the same as most schools, and everyone seems nice."

Q "Well, I can't really comment on the guys, but there are a lot of hot girls on campus. Girls vary, in terms of personality, though—**some are very sweet, and some are stuck up**."

Q "Well, I'm a real man's man—**I think any type of girl is hot!**"

Q "People at OSU are generally pretty cool. It's one of the biggest universities in the world, so **there are many different types of people**; you're bound to meet people you like, even though they may be completely different from you."

Q "There are definitely some hot guys here. **People here are a little preppy**, but pretty much every group you can imagine is represented here. There are people of all kinds."

Q "Go to the Oval on a warm day and **take your pick**."

Q "**The guys are fun**, and the girls are fun. My mom has commented before that the guys at Ohio State are infinitely hotter than at Ohio University."

Q "Oh yeah, the **guys are pretty hot**, if you can get 'em."

Q "There are so many people on campus that **you can find a type of person for all different tastes**. You will not have a problem finding attractive members of the opposite sex."

www.collegeprowler.com

GUYS & GIRLS | 71

The College Prowler Take On...
Guys & Girls

A campus as large as OSU's tends to make one optimistic in regards to finding someone attractive. Some students, of course, are taken, but there is also a large majority of available coeds who are out in search of a good time. Guys and girls alike feel that there is enough variety to find any type of relationship you're searching for. No matter what your style is, students agree that you can probably find your type somewhere on campus. It doesn't hurt that there are some 50,000 other people around the city, either.

Some students could care less about the selection—any willing partner will do. If this is the case, you're in good shape because of the sheer amount of people at OSU. If you are more selective, there will still be plenty who fit your profile. The feeling around campus is pretty upbeat, and there are many places to go searching for a specific type of girl or guy. Just look around you: classrooms and residence halls are a great place to meet people. It's also a good idea to go around town and hit the different scenes, because there is a lot of variety out there. Study dates are a great way to get to know someone in class a little better. On sunny days, put on your best clothes and take a stroll around campus. One piece of advice, guys: if you're around the Oval on a warm, sunny day, bring sunglasses; or at least, remember to blink once in awhile!

B+

The College Prowler® Grade on
Guys: B+

A high grade for Guys indicates that the male population on campus is attractive, smart, friendly, and engaging, and that the school has a decent ratio of guys to girls.

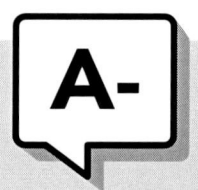

A-

The College Prowler® Grade on
Girls: A-

A high grade for Girls not only implies that the women on campus are attractive, smart, friendly, and engaging, but also that there is a fair ratio of girls to guys.

Athletics

The Lowdown On...
Athletics

Athletic Division:
Division I

Conference:
ECAC

School Mascot:
Brutus Buckeye

Males Playing Varsity Sports:
500 (3%)

Females Playing Varsity Sports:
415 (3%)

Men's Varsity Sports:
Baseball
Basketball
Cross-Country
Fencing
Football
Golf
Gymnastics
Ice Hockey
Lacrosse
Pistol/Rifle
Soccer
Swimming & Diving
Track & Field
Tennis
Volleyball
Wrestling

Women's Varsity Sports:
Baketball
Cross-Country
Fencing
Field Hockey
Golf
Gymnastics
Ice Hockey
Lacrosse
Pistol/Rifle
Rowing
Soccer
Softball
Swimming & Diving
Synchronized Swimming
Tennis
Track & Field
Volleyball

Club Sports:
Alpine Ski
Aikido
All Girl Cheer Team
Baseball
Basketball
Buckeye Dance Force
Buckeye Masters Swim
Buckeye Tang Soo Do
Crew
Cricket
Cycling
Do Jung Ishu
Dragon Phoenix Wushu
Drum Major/Twirling
Equestrian
Fast Pitch Softball
Field Hockey (Coed, Women's)
Figure Skating
Filipino Martial Arts
Gymnastics
Hapkido
Ice Hockey (Men's, Women's)
Isshin Ryu Karate
Ju Jutsu
Judo
Kendo Iaido
Kokikai Aikido
Korean Karate & Haedong
Kukki Taekwondo
Kumdo
Lacrosse (Men's, Women's)
Mountaineers
Law School Rugby
Paintball
Polo
Racquetball

(Club Sports, continued)
Roller Hockey
Rugby (Men's, Women's)
Running Club
Sailing
Scuba
Self-Defense (Women's)
Shito Ryu Karate
Shotokan Karate
Shuai Chiao Kungfu
Skydiving
Soccer (Men's, Women's)
Taekwondo
Tennis
Ultimate Disc (Men's, Women's)
Water Polo (Men's, Women's)
Volleyball (Men's, Women's)
Water Skiing
Wrestling

For more information on any of these sports, check: *www.ohiostaterecsports.org*

Intramurals:
4-On-4 Flag Football Tournament
Badminton
Basketball
Beat Michigan Week
Bench Press Competition
Buckeye World Games
Card Tournaments
College Flag Football Regional
Horseshoes
Ice Hockey
Indoor Volleyball
Inner Tube Water Polo
Jingle Bell Run
Match Play Golf
Nike/Big Ten 3-Point Shootout
Racquetball
Roller Hockey Tournament
Sand Volleyball Tournament
Soccer
Softball
Squash
Super Hoops 3-on-3 Tournament
Table Tennis
Volleyball
World Team Tennis
Wrestling

Athletic Fields

Bill Davis Stadium (baseball), Buckeye Field (softball), French Field House (indoor track & field), Jessie Owens Memorial Stadium (track & field, soccer, lacrosse), North Turf Field (field hockey), Ohio Stadium/the Horseshoe/the Shoe (football), OSU Ice Rink (women's ice hockey), Peppe Aquatic Center, Scarlet and Gray Golf Courses, Stickney Tennis Center, St. John Arena (women's basketball), and Value City Arena at the Jerome Schottenstein Center (men's basketball, men's ice hockey)

Getting Tickets

Every current student gets the option of pre-ordering season tickets for nearly every athletic program in the University. The most highly sought after are football tickets. Good luck scalping them, however. The tickets are now bar-coded, and before they are scanned to let you in, you must present your student ID. The cost of season tickets varies from sport to sport. Many sports charge no admission to watch. Be sure to check out women's lacrosse or men's soccer. Some charge a small amount, like men's ice hockey, and women's basketball and baseball. Not only do these sports charge small ticket fees, but they consistently compete for the league title. Check *www.hangonsloopy.com* for ticketing information.

Most Popular Sports

Football is king. Other sports on campus are popular, but none exceed the juggernaut that is football. Men's ice hockey enjoys a devoted following, and the basketball programs are top-notch. Don't forget about soccer or baseball, either.

Students Speak Out On...
Athletics

> **"Sports are kind of big, I guess, if you are an athletic person. Intramural sports are pretty cool and very easy to get into—lots of people do them."**

"**We are a Big Ten school**! Sports are huge, and we love the Buckeyes! Let me tell you, football games are the greatest—they're so much fun!"

"**Many people are involved in intramural sports**—there is something for everyone!"

"One of the largest intramural programs in the country gives any sports lover **the opportunity to compete in a wide variety of sports** at many different skill levels. From popular sports such as flag football or basketball, to the lesser-known inner tube water polo, OSU rec sports offer everyone the chance to play. And don't forget the best sport ever: ice hockey!"

"**Sports are huge, especially football**, but as a nonconformist, I prefer varsity ice hockey! A lot of people don't realize that we have a really kick-ass team with a ton of great guys, several of whom have already gone pro or are on their way. So, if you want to avoid the football hype and still enjoy a varsity sport, go the route of men's ice hockey."

"**OSU football and basketball are the best**! We have one of the biggest stadiums in college football, and on game days the atmosphere is awesome! The intramural sports are really cool, too."

Q "**Varsity sports are pretty huge, especially the way campus treats us**. We have wonderful training and workout facilities, including our own trainers, psychologists, and academic advisers. IM sports are pretty huge, too, because anyone can play. We have some pretty diverse ones, too, though I'm not really sure how popular inner tube water polo is."

Q "Varsity sports are huge, if by varsity sports you mean college football. **We have a lot of good athletic teams, men's and women's**, that don't receive the attention football receives, because half of the school population is still gloating about being the 2002 national champions of college football. Intramural sports are popular, the biggest being flag football, softball, soccer, and ice hockey."

Q "It's football heaven here in Columbus. **The people here love their Buckeyes** and support them through thick and thin. And who else can boast to have a player Archie Griffin who won not one, but two Heisman Trophies?"

Q "Varsity sports are big. **Everyone goes out and cheers for our teams**, especially football. Intramural sports, however, are where it's at. You definitely need to participate in the intramural sports, no matter what your athletic ability is. I especially recommend ice hockey. I can hardly skate, but it's a blast! And the champions get a T-shirt!"

The College Prowler Take On...
Athletics

Football, football, football! You'll be hard-pressed to find a more competitive football school than OSU, the 2002 national champions. Through the football team, Ohio State has managed to start rivalries with nearly every other team in the Big Ten. Columbus is filled with block parties and huge crowds getting ready for each game, and competition is always high. The varsity football team is complimented by a number of other successful varsity sports—from the pistol and rifle team, to track and field or soccer, Ohio State fields the best that the state has to offer.

Despite the prevalence of football, don't forget that there are many other sports at all levels. There are great baseball, basketball, and gymnastics programs, along with many others. An abundance of intramural sports keeps the physically active students busy, as well. OSU intramurals offer nearly every type of sport you can think of (and probably some that you can't), all at varied skill levels. Just be careful when dealing with the Department of Recreational Sports—the slightest violation could get you suspended for a quarter of intramural sports, if not more. A great sport to try is D-league intramural ice hockey; even if you've never set foot on ice in your entire life, you will be right at home in this league. When playing an intramural sport, always keep in mind that the officials are just students like you. At games, paint your face, wear your Buckeye necklace, and sing Carmen Ohio at the top of your lungs as you attend the games. Ohio State sports are all about tradition, and the next chapter is always being written.

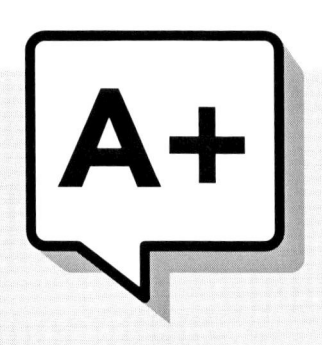

The College Prowler® Grade on Athletics: A+

A high grade in Athletics indicates that students have school spirit, that sports programs are respected, that games are well-attended, and that intramurals are a prominent part of student life.

Nightlife

The Lowdown On...
Nightlife

Club and Bar Prowler: Popular Nightlife Spots!

Having so many clubs so close to a college campus means that they get much more packed than a regular town's clubs. College students mainly fill them, but there is also a handful of non-students, too.

Most places are 21 and up only. This excludes a lot of minors from even entering the bar let alone get served a drink.

The Brewery District in downtown Columbus is overrun by bars. The Gateway project on South Campus promises to bring new nightlife to the area, if and when it is ever completed.

Blue Danube
2439 N. High St.
(614) 261-9308

One of the only places to get some grub after midnight, Blue Danube is a popular hang out for OSU students, and it would be a rare night to go here without knowing a handful of people. What we love most about the "Dube" is that it's cheap, and it gives us what we want: beer and finger foods. Hipsters and jocks alike will agree that this is the place to be—music preferences aside.

Dick's Den
2417 N. High St.
(614) 268-9573

Looks like a college bar, but it doesn't quite sound like a college bar. Jazz music radiates into the blistering cold nights, as trumpets and saxes woo patrons into a drunken stupor, while they sip down another strong, cheap vodka drink. Glorious, I say, glorious!

The Distillery/Bernie's Bagels
1896 N. High St.
(614) 291-3448

Indie rock started here—no, not exactly, but Beck did play here back in the day. Students come here in the daytime for coffee and bagels, and come back at night for live local bands, as well as nationally touring bands seven days a week.

Four Kegs
12 E. 15th Ave.
(614) 298-8000

Located on the intersection of frat row and High Street, I'll give you three guesses as to who frequents this popular bar, (no, it's not your mom). Great drink specials and a kicking jukebox, just as long as you like "Piano Man" and "Friends in Low Places." Oh, and there's an outdoor patio, which is great for people-watching in warm weather.

High Five Bar & Grill
1227 N. High St.
(614) 421-2998

www.highfivebar.com

Good microbrew menu, as well as beers from around the world. Menu is good for all you munchers, with half-off burgers on Tuesdays, 2-for-1 pizzas on Thursdays, $5 fish and chips on Fridays, and double orders of cheesesticks, wings, and hummus for the price of one on Sundays. Monday is punk karaoke night, Tuesday there is no cover and $3 Washington Apple martinis, Wednesday is entertainment appreciation day with half-off Guinness, Thursday $5 bomb drinks, Fridays $2 New Castle drafts, Saturdays $5 Black Hole martinis, and Sundays features $2.50 pints of Bells. Happy hour is Monday–Friday 5 p.m.–9 p.m. with $1 domestic and well drinks. Drinkers, drink on.

Larry's

2040 N. High St.

(614) 299-6010

www.larrysbar.com

Voted "best place to drown your sorrows" and runner-up for "best jukebox" in *Columbus Alive*, Larry's offers artwork, poetry, a great happy hour daily until 9 p.m. on selected drinks from $1.50 frozen margaritas to $1.50 microbrews or gin and tonics. Hours are: Saturday–Sunday
5 p.m.–2:30 a.m.,
Monday–Wednesday, Friday
4 p.m.–2:30 a.m., and
Thursday 1 p.m.–2:30 a.m.

Little Brother's

1100 N. High St.

(614) 421-2032 general

(614) 421-2025 show info

www.littlebrothers.com

Committed to small-venue music scenes, Little Brother's attracts local bands with covers of $2–$5, and in the past has featured mainstream groups such as the Wallflowers, 10,000 Maniacs, Nirvana, and the Red Hot Chili Peppers. Check Web site for ticketing and scheduling inquiries, or visit Ticketmaster to purchase tickets for upcoming shows.

Newport Music Hall

1722 N. High St.

(614) 294-1659

This venue has all the fixings for a classic rock show. Its cathedral build, balcony and "dark" setting gives it all the character in the world. The artists seem to perform more naturally here than in a big, shiny, new venue. The Newport "keeps it real," if such a term still exists! Newport serves expensive domestic beers in plastic cups, and you're right up close to the bands you love, such as 311 and Steve Earl!

Northberg Tavern

2084 N. High St.

(614) 421-3667

Northberg feels like a hole in the wall, with wood paneling, vinyl chairs, and a constant haze of smoke billowing over patrons' heads, yet its location (under Donato's Pizza) and its entertainment make its popularity undeniable.

Out-R-Inn

20 E. Frambes Ave.

(614) 294-9259

Only blocks from Ohio Stadium and Value City Arena, sports fans flock here, especially to root the Buckeyes on. This bar has two outdoor patios, four dart boards, six pool tables, a few basketball games, and $1 drafts on Sundays.

Red Zone
303 S Front St.
(614) 621-0416
www.redzone-club.com

The best hip hop club in Columbus, Red Zone is popular because of its comfortable lounge seating and its jam-packed dance floors. Red Zone features three different dance floors/lounges, with appearances made by internationally-known DJs. This club is for the young, sophisticated, fabulous crowd.

Varsity Club
278 W. Lane Ave.
(614) 299-6269

Wondering where you will be pre- and post-gaming on Ohio State game nights? Uh, that'll be the Varsity Club. Forget who you're rooting for? No worries, because the place is packed with OSU memorabilia.

Student Favorites:
Four Kegs, Larry's, Red Zone

Bars Close At:
2 a.m.

Primary Areas with Nightlife:
Downtown Columbus

Cheapest Place to Get a Drink:
Larry's

What to Do if You're Not 21:
Go to a club, hit an off-campus party, or catch a concert.

Favorite Drinking Games:
Beer Pong
Card Games
Century Club
Cornhole
Flip Cup
Power Hour
Quarters

Organization Parties:
Individual organizations have get-togethers at different times during the year. If you're interested, check out one of the meetings.

Frats:
See the Greek section!

Students Speak Out On...
Nightlife

"Campus Partners completely wiped out the entire South Campus bar district leaving nothing standing. This has totally dampened the 'party-crazy' stigma of the South Campus residents."

Q "**Red Zone is awesome**. They have really revamped the place from the slum I remember. Now, it's actually a decent place to shake your groove thing!"

Q "I'm not 21 yet, so I haven't really checked out the bars, but I'm a musician, so I've checked out a lot of good clubs. In particular, Little Brother's, the Northberg Tavern, and the Newport Music Club are **great for live bands**."

Q "**Bars and clubs are being revamped around campus**. The new trend is to head to bars downtown. There is pretty much any type of club or bar that you could ask for."

Q "The only **good bars are all off campus**."

Q "**There is never a weekend without a good party**, and most people are very friendly. You can pretty much participate in any party, especially if you're a girl. The bars have pretty much disappeared, thanks to Campus Partners."

Q "Bars suck, plain and simple. There aren't that many, those that do exist **tend to be overcrowded** and not all that fun. I miss the days of table dancing at Panini's!"

Q "**The parties are generally really big and really loud**, and alcohol is more abundant than water. I can't tell you about bars and clubs, though, because those places bore me."

Q "What happened to the South Campus bars? **They're all gone now, because of that vile Campus Partners thing**; just thinking about it gets me so mad!"

Q "The Brewery District in Downtown Columbus has a **massive selection of bars that really appeals to anyone** who is 21 and older."

The College Prowler Take On...
Nightlife

The demolition of the South Campus bars by Campus Partners, a University-affiliated non-profit civic association in 2002 has really hindered the *"Animal House"* appeal of the area. This should change when their urban revitalization project is completed, however. The only bars and small clubs which are left around the campus can be found on the North Side. Many students frequent local bars such as Four Kegs and Red Zone. Because of the diminished scene, those who frequent these clubs and bars are a little more united. Larry's, a bar that recently celebrated it 70th anniversary, enjoys a devoted following, as well.

The main attraction, as far as clubs and bars are concerned, resides in downtown Columbus. The Brewery District, along with various other clubs, has transformed downtown into a perennial hotspot. This area is mostly 21 and up, however, which makes it off-limits for a lot of students at OSU. If you're underage or can't make it downtown, your best bet is a house party off campus for drinks and dancing. The club scene is definitely not big on weekends. Follow the loud noise and packs of freshmen traveling together, and you're likely to run across at least one or two big parties.

B+

The College Prowler® Grade on
Nightlife: B+

A high grade in Nightlife indicates that there are many bars and clubs in the area that are easily accessible and affordable. Other determining factors include the number of options for the under-21 crowd and the prevalence of house parties.

Greek Life

The Lowdown On...
Greek Life

Number of Fraternities:
40

Number of Sororities:
19

Undergrad Men in Fraternities:
6%

Undergrad Females in Sororities:
7%

Fraternities:
Acacia
Alpha Epsilon Pi
Alpha Gamma Rho
Alpha Gamma Sigma
Alpha Phi Alpha
Alpha Psi Lambda
Alpha Sigma Phi
Alpha Tau Omega
Alpha Tau Zeta
Beta Kappa Gamma
Beta Theta Pi
Chi Phi
Delta Chi
Delta Lambda Phi
Delta Tau Delta
Delta Theta Sigma
Delta Upsilon
Evans Scholars
Iota Phi Theta
Kappa Alpha Psi
Kappa Sigma
Lambda Chi Alpha
Omega Psi Phi
Phi Delta Theta
Phi Gamma Delta
Phi Kappa Psi
Phi Kappa Tau
Phi Kappa Theta
Pi Delta Psi
Pi Kappa Alpha
Sigma Alpha Epsilon
Sigma Alpha Mu
Sigma Chi
Sigma Epsilon Phi
Sigma Phi Epsilon
Tau Kappa Epsilon
Theta Tau
Theta Xi
Triangle
Zeta Beta Tau

Sororities:
Alpha Chi Omega
Alpha Epsilon Phi
Alpha Gamma Delta
Alpha Omicron Pi
Alpha Phi
Alpha Xi Delta
Chi Omega
Delta Delta Delta
Delta Gamma
Delta Sigma Theta
Delta Zeta
Kappa Alpha Theta
Kappa Delta
Kappa Kappa Gamma
Kappa Phi Lambda
Omega Tau Zeta
Phi Sigma Rho
Pi Beta Phi
Zeta Phi Beta

Other Greek Organizations:
The Panhellenic Council and special groups for specific fields of study are also a part of OSU Greek life. For Intrafraternity Council, check out: *http://osugreeks.com/ifc*.

Multicultural Colonies:
OSU has a number of multicultural organizations and programs, based out of the Multicultural Center at the Ohio Union. Check out the Multicultural Center's Web site, *http://multiculturalcenter.osu.edu*, for an up-to-date list of organizations and activities.

Students Speak Out On...
Greek Life

"Personally, I'm kind of anti-Greek (against the frats and sororities themselves, though, not the people). It definitely doesn't dominate the social scene."

"**Greek life is definitely not necessary**; in fact, it is almost frowned upon by a lot of people. Those who are Greek usually are extremely busy with all of the stuff they deal with. The parties are fun to go to once in a while, though, and they have free beer!"

"I am a member of Chi Omega sorority. I think its good to get involved, and **I really have a fun time with my sorority** sisters. Greek life is not essential to your experience at Ohio State, but I think it's worth doing."

"The fraternities and sororities are **just about nonexistent**."

"For some, **Greek life is a big part of the social scene**, for others, it's not. It's not dominating."

"I have no clue, but **sororities suck up your life**."

"There is a **healthy population of Greek life at OSU**, but in my opinion, it does not dominate the social scene. There are so many things to get involved with—it just depends on your interest. Some people come to OSU wanting to be in the Greek system, other people don't ever want to be involved in it. With so many students, it is really diverse, and people will not look down upon you at all if you don't join."

Q "**Greek life is all over, although I am not part of it**. I belong to one of the technical sororities on campus, which has a lot of the benefits of belonging to a social sorority without any of the negatives.'"

Q "Not much attention is placed on frats or sororities—I think the majority of the people confuse it with what they see in the movies. Believe me when I tell you, **Greek life is nothing like that in reality**."

Q "I don't care about Greek life. I'd shoot myself if I was in a fraternity. I hate **so-called Greek 'life!'**"

Q "**It isn't a 'must' for you to join** a Greek house to fit in. You can just use them for their great parties. That's what I always do."

The College Prowler Take On...
Greek Life

An overwhelming majority of students agree that being part of a fraternity or sorority isn't a necessary part of your experience at OSU. In fact, many students look down on Greek organizations, and sometimes on those who join them. One of the biggest problems with OSU's Greek life is its lack of real contribution to the city. That, along with many violations and infractions (that can put a Greek house in probationary status), doesn't bode well for their image. The houses may look magnificent along the streets off campus, but for many, their appeal stops at the door.

There's a lot of temptation to join a fraternity or sorority when you first get to school, and many of the Greek organizations will actively try to recruit from the incoming class. Remember that Greek status isn't necessary to have an active social life at OSU, however. Many choose to join for the parties alone, though you don't necessarily have to be in a fraternity or sorority to party with them. If you're looking for service activities, however, there are some organizations that do this well. Tau Beta Pi, for instance, puts on the annual "Beat Michigan 5K" (*www.beatmichigan5k.org*) race to raise funds for a local food pantry. Overall, however, Greek Life occupies a very specific niche at OSU; if you're not sure whether or not it's for you, it's wise to check out what the Greeks have to say, and talk to other students about the image and opportunities that come along with a fraternity or sorority. If nothing else, there's probably a free T-shirt in it for you.

The College Prowler® Grade on

A high grade in Greek Life indicates that sororities and fraternities are not only present, but also active on campus. Other determining factors include the variety of houses available and the respect the Greek community receives from the rest of the campus.

Drug Scene

The Lowdown On...
Drug Scene

Most Prevalent Drugs on Campus:
Alcohol
Marijuana

Liquor-Related Referrals and Arrests:
617

Drug-Related Referrals and Arrests:
172

Drug Counseling Programs

Alcoholics Anonymous

(614) 253-8501

AA offers help for people of all genders and creeds to achieve and maintain sobriety.

Crossroads Recovery Services

(614) 445-0352 or (614) 582-4885

Offers assistance for drug, alcohol, marijuana, and domestic violence problems, among others, as well as weekend programs for DUI offenders.

Focus Health Care

(614) 885-1944

Offers intensive outpatient services for drug abuse.

The John C. Wilce Student Health Center

(614) 292-4527

http://swc.osu.edu

The Student Health Center offers counseling, drug abuse prevention, and a medical staff.

OSU Counseling & Consultation Services

(614) 292-5766

Provides counseling and consultation services to currently enrolled undergraduate and graduate students and their spouses/partners. Offers brief counseling and therapy to help students address personal, academic, and career concerns. Both individual and group counseling are available.

Students Speak Out On...
Drug Scene

> "There is drug use, of course; I mean, this is a huge university. However, there aren't junkies running around. The most common drug is pot."

- "Drugs aren't a big problem. **Alcohol use and abuse is honestly much more of a concern**."

- "**I haven't seen any drugs since I got here**, but I'm sure they're out there."

- "**Two words: Hemp Fest**. It's out there, baby."

- "This is **mostly a drinking campus**."

- "**Every campus has drugs**. I don't feel as though it is a big problem here."

- "**Drugs here are expensive compared to back home**. That's why I'm not doing anything here. Drugs don't run rampant, though. In fact, there aren't that many potheads around. The real drug of choice here is booze."

- "I'm not into drugs, and I never have been, so **I really don't know what the drug scene is like**. I just know that I stay away from it."

- "**There is a drug scene on campus**, but you have to want to find it. If you're not into that stuff, then it probably won't be a big deal at all. If you're into that stuff, it's around. Some things are easier to get then others."

Q "**Marijuana is plentiful**. It makes an appearance at most parties. If you're looking to avoid drugs, though, don't worry; no one will force you to do them."

Q "There is nothing really noteworthy here, and **aside from the hippies, there isn't really a drug scene** that overtakes the campus—which is a good thing."

Q "**They've got crappy acid, even crappier ecstasy**! The drugs here in Columbus suck major eggs!"

The College Prowler Take On...
Drug Scene

Alcohol is, by far, the most prevalent drug on the OSU campus. The rest of the drug scene isn't terribly huge, and it is kept in check by factors such as price, since students claim that drugs around OSU are more expensive than most places. There are also complaints from certain students about the actual potency of the drugs in the area. Overall, this has been enough to keep it out of the primary social atmosphere. You can find the scene if you're looking for it, but it's not something you're likely to run across by accident (with the possible exception of marijuana).

Marijuana seems to be the drug that always shows up, but to OSU's credit, this happens at nearly every campus. The legalization debate pops up frequently on campus, and "Hemp Fest" takes place each spring on the South Oval (you can get a serious contact high just from walking within a block of it). There are also constant campus flyers for events where you can win free water pipes. While this marijuana subculture isn't officially supported in any way, it is pretty evident; however, it is also quite easy to avoid, and there isn't any social pressure. Stoners tend to band together and not go to class. Outside of the pot crowd, there isn't any readily available or evident drug market, and little to worry about beyond the ever-present alcohol.

B

The College Prowler® Grade on Drug Scene: B

A high grade in the Drug Scene indicates that drugs are not a noticeable part of campus life; drug use is not visible, and no pressure to use them seems to exist.

Campus Strictness

The Lowdown On...
Campus Strictness

What Are You Most Likely to Get Caught Doing on Campus?
- Underage drinking
- Illegal parking
- Public intoxication
- Indecent exposure
- Lighting candles in your room
- Playing music too loud
- Public urination
- Disorderly conduct
- Not respecting "courtesy hours"

Students Speak Out On...
Campus Strictness

> "The whole city is very strict about alcohol. Be careful at bars and parties when you're drinking, because you never know where undercover cops are. Take it from me: be very careful about using a fake ID in a bar."

Q "Basically, as long as you are partying safely, the police really don't care. **Most bars have been strict about underage people drinking**, but I think you'll find that everywhere."

Q "There are state and federal laws, but the **cops are a little lax on drinking** because they know everyone does it."

Q "I'm an RA, and **I absolutely love busting people** with things that they know are illegal."

Q "**Campus police do their job**. So if you're smoking something you shouldn't, they won't just turn their heads. Same goes for other drugs, of course."

Q "Police suck! **They are pretty strict about drinking** and stuff, but at the same time, they will always give you a warning before you get busted."

Q "**Columbus police are strict about drugs and riots**. If you get caught for underage drinking at a bar, it can be a serious punishment, but the police are very laid-back about house parties."

- "Just remember kids—whatever you do, **don't jaywalk**!"

- "If you take your activities to the east side of High Street and avoid the really big, wild parties, **you can usually do whatever you want**. The police generally look the other way."

- "**They don't mess around**."

- "**They aren't as strict as I thought they would be**, especially with pot in the dorms. You just get written up for it, which means absolutely nothing."

The College Prowler Take On...
Campus Strictness

Though students often disagree about the strictness of University regulations, there is no denying that you can and will get arrested if you're causing a disturbance or are heavily under the influence of an illegal substance. Most cops and University police will issue warnings before an actual arrest, but don't take this for leniency. If any type of law enforcement officer gives you a warning, consider yourself lucky and change your ways. Given OSU's past history of misconduct and rioting, it's understandable that security will come down hard on anyone they believe to be a threat to public safety.

The residence halls strictly regulate access—after 9 p.m., you cannot get into any hall other than your own (or any hall at all, if you live off campus). RAs will generally let you do your own thing, though, provided you're not disturbing anyone else. The best thing to keep in mind is courtesy to those around you; even if you don't have an 8 a.m. class, the girl living below you might. Excessive noise is one of the easiest ways to get caught breaking the rules by an RA, and you can actually be evicted for too many violations. While University police are relatively lax, it's not wise to push the boundaries. Officers will hesitate to arrest an underage student who has had one or two alcoholic beverages, since they would be setting a difficult standard to follow; if you're causing a public disturbance, however, they won't waste any time singling you out. Strictness is nothing to worry about at OSU, provided you keep your partying to a reasonable level.

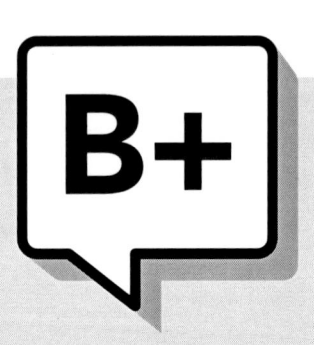

B+

The College Prowler® Grade on
Campus Strictness: B+

A high Campus Strictness grade implies an overall lenient atmosphere; police and RAs are fairly tolerant, and the administration's rules are flexible.

Parking

The Lowdown On...
Parking

Approximate Parking Permit Cost:
$40

OSU Transportation and Parking:
160 Bevis Hall
1080 Carmack Road
Columbus, OH 43210
(614) 292-9341
www.tp.ohio-state.edu

Common Parking Tickets:
Expired Meter: $25
Failure to Display Permit: $3
Handicapped Zone: $150
No Parking Zone: $35
Parked Out Of Zone: $30–$50
Unauthorized Use of a Parking Permit: $150

Student Parking Lot?
Yes

Freshmen Allowed to Park?
No

Parking Permits

"A" Permit – Faculty only

"B" Permit – Staff and graduate students

"C" Permit – Commuter students (rank 3 or 4)

"WC" Permit – Commuter students

"WC5" Permit – All others

The higher up the hierarchy your pass is, the more parking options you have. "A" permits can park anywhere, anytime, while "WC5" permits are relegated to the West-Campus parking lots, on the other side of the Olentangy River from campus.

Did You Know?

Best Places to Find a Parking Spot

The West Campus lots, near the Stadium.

Good Luck Getting a Parking Spot Here!

During the day, pretty much anywhere. Don't even try on South Campus unless you have an "A" permit.

Students Speak Out On...
Parking

> "Parking is horrible around here. There's not enough of it, and it's all far away. Transportation and Parking Services also hands out lots of tickets."

Q "**Most freshmen park over on West Campus**. It's far away, but your car is safe there. You have to buy a pass, too."

Q "If you're coming from out of town, all you have to do is bring your car, buy a permit, and park on West Campus. It's safe for the most part, but there have been a few cases of people stealing car radios. If you're just driving around campus, it's not easy to park, and **it is very easy to get your car towed**. The towing fee here is close to $120, so be careful!"

Q "At times, **it can be difficult to park on campus**— especially on football weekends."

Q "The University really doesn't give parking preference to students. A good example? They give out North Campus' main weekend lot to tailgaters on game day, leaving us with about 50 spots to split. Don't wanna wait half an hour for the bus at the West Campus lots by yourself in the dark? **It's either that or get a $70 ticket and tow**."

Q "Parking sucks! I will not give away my secrets on where to park now that I've got them all figured out, but just a warning, **they like to ticket and tow here**. Ask me who lost close to $300 in parking tickets last year!"

Q "If you live off campus, **live close enough to walk to class if you can**."

Q "**I think it's a big pain to park around here**. There are not many free parking spots. Don't bring your car unless you think you absolutely can't live without it. I have had no problems here without a car this year."

Q "Parking sucks—**there's no two ways about it**!"

Q "Plain and simply put: **OSU gives out a lot of tickets**!"

Q "The parking on campus is horrendous. **They sell as many passes as there are people**. So there are probably over a thousand more people than there are parking spaces. The school makes enough money alone off of parking permits and parking tickets that they could fund a parking garage to be built."

The College Prowler Take On...
Parking

Parking at OSU is a task in itself, and when you do find a spot, it will probably be quite a distance from campus. While the University has tried to add more parking lots, the sheer number of students and prospective students makes it impossible for everyone to keep a vehicle on campus. In addition, some spots are getting lost to construction or taken over for events such as football tailgating, worsening an already bad situation. You will get at least one parking ticket in four years.

Students are not allowed to park on campus itself during the day, and overnight parking isn't legal. If you have a parking permit you can try the student parking on West Campus, but you'll have to take your chances everywhere else. The bottom line: get ready to build some leg muscles—you're going to find yourself walking just about everywhere. Generally speaking, it isn't even worth bringing a vehicle to campus. It's a hassle driving back and forth from the West Campus lot, and you can't count on parking anywhere else. In addition, all the main stores and campus buildings are well within walking distance. For getting around at OSU, the on-campus transportation system (CABS) is fairly efficient, with routes to get you almost everywhere you'll need to go. If you don't feel like waiting for the bus, you can always walk; traffic is so bad, it often doesn't save time to go places by vehicle, anyway.

The College Prowler® Grade on Parking: C-

A high grade in this section indicates that parking is both available and affordable, and that parking enforcement isn't overly severe.

Transportation

The Lowdown On...
Transportation

Ways to Get Around Town:

On Campus

Campus Area Bus System (CABS)
(614) 292-6122

The OSU busing system, CABS, offers routes for students and visitors while on campus.

For a list of what routes are run and when, check:

www.tp.ohio-state.edu/cabs

Taxi Cabs

Acme Taxi
(614) 777-7777

A Cab
(614) 262-3333

Acme Taxi
(614) 299-9990

Airport Taxi Service
(614) 868-8888

Arch Transportation
(614) 252-2277

Arlington-Grandview
(614) 486-2432

Arlington GS Kab King
(614) 488-0111

(Taxis, continued)

Bobcat Cab Service
(614) 481-0388

Buckeye Corporate
Transportation
(614) 848-9863

Central Ohio Shuttle
(614) 291-9999

Certified Network
Columbus Taxi
(614) 447-8366

Ways to Get Out of Town:

Airlines Serving Columbus

Continental
(800) 523-3273
www.continental.com

Delta
(800) 221-1212
www.delta.com

Northwest
(800) 225-2525
www.nwa.com

Southwest
(800) 435-9792
www.southwest.com

US Airways
(800) 428-4322
www.usairways.com

Airport

Port Columbus International
Airport, (614) 239-4000

www.port-columbus.com

The Columbus Airport is 10 miles and approximately a 15-minute drive from campus, depending on traffic.

How to Get To the Airport

From campus, take I-71 South to 670-West. Get off at the airport exit.

From the north, I-71 South to I-270 East, follow I-270 to exit #35.

From the west, I-70 East to I-71 North, follow I-71 to I-670 East, take I-670 to exit #9.

From the south, I-71 North to I-270 East, follow I-270 to exit #35.

From the east, I-70 West to I-270 North, follow I-270 to exit #35.

Students Speak Out On...
Transportation

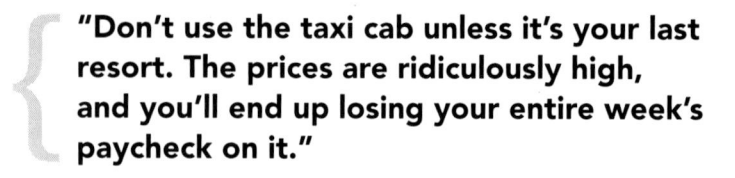

> "Don't use the taxi cab unless it's your last resort. The prices are ridiculously high, and you'll end up losing your entire week's paycheck on it."

Q "**Buses are the only public transportation**. The University automatically takes $10 in tuition so you can ride for free. The buses are always on schedule, and they can take you all sorts of places."

Q "**The CABS line is primarily used around campus**—just in case you need to get all the way to the other side of campus early in the morning."

Q "**Cabs are expensive**, try and avoid them if possible."

Q "**The COTA line goes to Easton** and even all the way to the airport. Make sure you get a pamphlet that shows you their specific routes because the last thing you want to do is get lost in them."

Q "I would never use the bus system—**there's a bunch of nasty people who use them**. It's so gross that it makes me sick just thinking about it."

Q "On-campus transportation is pretty good. **There are buses running all week, at most hours**. As for off campus, the city buses are somewhat unreliable. I don't use them that much, because I usually walk or drive. We don't have a subway or train system, although it would be nice!"

The College Prowler Take On...
Transportation

The general feeling is that the bus lines (COTA and CABS) are dependable. Some students have negative attitudes toward these services, perhaps because of the occasional delays that do happen; overall, though, the buses are reliable if you allow enough extra time. The COTA buses are one of the most useful transit options available to students. While you can usually walk anywhere on campus, making CABS service somewhat redundant, the COTA buses can open up areas of Columbus that you may otherwise not get to explore.

At first, the city buses can seem a little intimidating. Some students are afraid of the "scary" sorts of people that frequently use the system, and there's no denying that this element takes some getting used to. Where else will you meet these great, larger-than-life characters, though? Once you've ridden enough to get past the initial jitters, you'll be fine; the usefulness of the bus system makes it worthwhile. The #2 bus is the main line used to move students back and forth through Columbus, and the #84 takes students back to the Lennox and is also frequented by students. Make sure you catch the correct bus back to OSU, however; if you take the wrong one, it will loop far west before it gets to campus, and your trip will take well over an hour. Until you're sure of the schedules, stay in an area that you can walk back from—it's not hard to do around campus.

B+

The College Prowler® Grade on Transportation: B+

A high grade for Transportation indicates that campus buses, public buses, cabs, and rental cars are readily-available and affordable. Other determining factors include proximity to an airport and the necessity of transportation.

Weather

The Lowdown On...
Weather

Average Temperature:
Fall: 54 °F
Winter: 26 °F
Spring: 51 °F
Summer: 73 °F

Average Precipitation:
Fall: 10.02 in.
Winter: 12.42 in.
Spring: 8.42 in.
Summer: 7.66 in.

Students Speak Out On...
Weather

> **"Winter isn't that great. Now, why is that? Well, because all of the hot girls seem to hibernate like freakin' bears when it starts getting cold out."**

Q "**The weather is finicky**! One day it will be 80 degrees and sunny, and the next day it'll be 40 degrees and cloudy. It also rains a lot."

Q "This is Ohio; usually, the weather's okay, but **it has the tendency to be wacky sometimes**."

Q "Last time my boyfriend and I had this wonderful—and I mean wonderful—picnic planned out for nearly the entire day. The forecast said it would nice, clear skies the entire day, but just as I was getting everything set, a downpour ruined all of my plans. **The weather here is terrible**!"

Q "**There isn't that much snow during winter**. It's mostly cold and gray, which really sucks."

Q "**Bring a nice umbrella** (you won't look dorky—you'll be envied), comfortable shoes, a bathing suit, and shoes to wear in the snow."

Q "**Weather here is crazy**."

Q "As the radio weather guy on *The Simpsons* put it: 'Rain, changing to freezing rain, changing to sleet, changing to snow, and melting into spring.' We have **40 degree temperature drops within the span of a day**."

Q "It's beautiful in the spring, beautiful in the summer, pretty nice in the fall, and **usually cold during winter**."

Q "You could be wearing your triple-thick jacket in the morning and trying to catch some UV rays later on in the afternoon. **It's that crazy**!"

Q "Ohio can never seem to decide on a weather pattern. **Bring all types of clothes**: long sleeves, short sleeves, heavy and lightweight pants. You can never be too prepared; you will need all types of clothes here."

Q "It's Ohio—bring everything. **You never know what you're going to get**."

Q "The weather is really strange. **It could rain at a moment's notice**—which isn't always a bad thing. I remember having to go along with some little picnic of my girlfriend's one time, but just as I was about to force one of her terrible sandwiches down my throat the rain totally crashed down and ruined her parade. It was wickedly awesome, but I felt a little bad afterwards."

Q "Let's just leave it at this: **the weatherman is has his work cut out for him.**"

The College Prowler Take On...
Weather

Columbus has unpredictable weather, but the winter especially puts a damper on everyone's spirit. There isn't much to do while you're stuck in the worst snowstorms. It can be very difficult to plan things in advance with the unstable climate, especially outdoor things. Weather can change dramatically even during a single day—it's not uncommon for a cool morning rain to give way to a warm, sunny afternoon, or vice versa. The word "inconsistent" is the best way to sum up OSU's climate.

Weather may be one of the major things you'll need to accustom yourself to—especially if you're coming from a warm climate. Don't be surprised if you have to trek to class through the snow on many winter mornings. Remember to buy a warm jacket, and if you really need it, stock up on thermal underwear. Everyone agrees that you must be prepared for anything Mother Nature can throw at you, because around Columbus, she likes to mix things up. Huge temperature changes can happen in a single day, too, so the key word for clothing is "layers." Aside from the initial 4–5 months of winter weather, however, there is nothing but sunshine and rain; the climate can be beautiful, especially if you're staying over the summer. Take plenty of vitamins, though—your immune system will need all the help it can get adapting to the weather changes. Some years back, Ohio State received so much snowfall that classes were actually cancelled for a day for the first time in over 20 years. To hammer home the point of unpredictability—the year before, it only snowed once.

C+

The College Prowler® Grade on Weather: C+

A high Weather grade designates that temperatures are mild and rarely reach extremes, that the campus tends to be sunny rather than rainy, and that weather is fairly consistent rather than unpredictable.

OHIO STATE UNIVERSITY
Report Card Summary

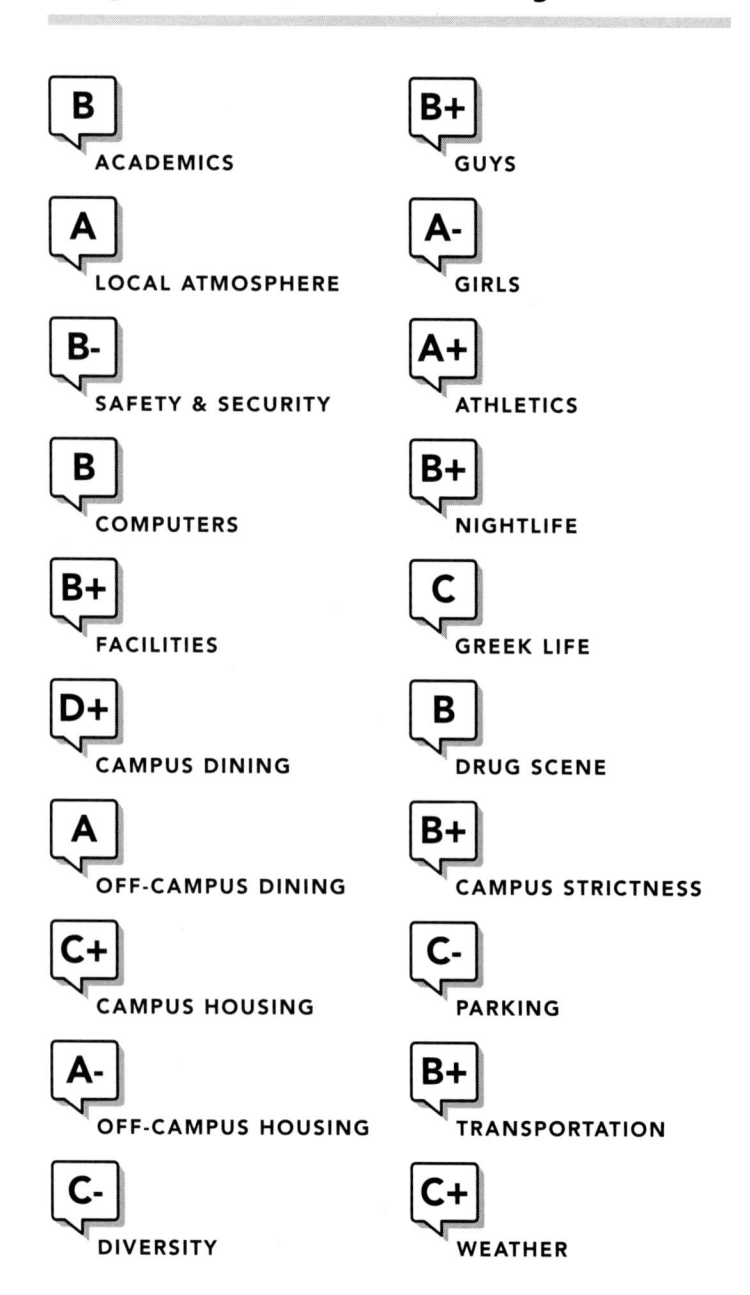

B ACADEMICS

A LOCAL ATMOSPHERE

B- SAFETY & SECURITY

B COMPUTERS

B+ FACILITIES

D+ CAMPUS DINING

A OFF-CAMPUS DINING

C+ CAMPUS HOUSING

A- OFF-CAMPUS HOUSING

C- DIVERSITY

B+ GUYS

A- GIRLS

A+ ATHLETICS

B+ NIGHTLIFE

C GREEK LIFE

B DRUG SCENE

B+ CAMPUS STRICTNESS

C- PARKING

B+ TRANSPORTATION

C+ WEATHER

Overall Experience

Students Speak Out On...
Overall Experience

"I love OSU. The entire athletic program has really made it memorable for me so far. Hopefully, we can continue representing and winning throughout my tenure here in school, because I would sure like to go out with my team on top."

"**I can't even imagine having gone anywhere else**. This university has provided me with so many opportunities that no other place could have given me. Ohio State will always be a part of who I am."

"I really like OSU! **It's a great school with a lot to offer**, and I believe that it is definitely the choice for me."

Q "Ohio State is amazing; it's the perfect college for me. I've visited other places, and there is no place that I'd rather be. **Ohio State encompasses all aspects of the college experience**. It's a place where you'll make your best friends, you'll meet people from all walks of life, and even learn a thing or two. It definitely offers a unique and totally liberating college experience to all who bear the scarlet and gray."

Q "I like OSU's big campus. **It's made me more social**, and I've found some really good friends that I know will be a part of my life, now and for years to come. There are so many new bonds I have forged that I feel very happy with my decision to come here."

Q "I love Ohio State. I didn't even apply to another school. **Everyone here has so much school spirit**, it's almost sickening. When you hear "Hang On Sloopy" at a house party, everyone starts cheering for OSU."

Q "I loved OSU, and I am **thrilled to call myself an OSU alumnus**."

Q "I love it here. **I wouldn't want to be anywhere else**. I can tell you where I wouldn't want to be, though, and that's Ann Arbor, Michigan."

Q "My overall experience has been a good one. I have met some great people and **enjoyed the benefits of being a student-athlete**. I transferred from Denver, and everyone asks me why I came to Ohio, but even now, thinking back, I'm still glad I transferred. I do not regret making that decision. I have seen another part of the nation, and there was definitely a culture shock that has taken some time to get used to. I wouldn't trade my college experience here in Ohio for anything."

Q "So far, I love it here. It has its negatives, but overall, the experience is great. I've met some wonderful people, and **there are so many options class-wise**. There's always something going on for you to get involved in. Ohio people are very friendly (almost too much so). I don't think I could live in Ohio forever, but OSU is definitely a fun place to be."

Q "It's a really big school, so if you like a lot of personal attention and hand holding, this probably isn't the place for you. But if you want a big school with **lots of choices and options**, this may be a good place for you."

The College Prowler Take On...
Overall Experience

There is a reason the Buckeye Nation is considered to be so devoted; an overwhelming love for OSU is evident in student responses, and in the loyalty of alumni to their alma mater. Each person has his or her own reasons for loving the University, and there are quite a few of them. Some students feel that the academics are top-notch and have found exactly the programs they wanted; others lean toward the athletic success of the Buckeye teams, while some just feel that the friendships and bonds they have made are enough to make their tenure at OSU worthwhile. At any rate, everyone can agree that being a Buckeye creates a special bond between you and nearly 50,000 other students, which you will carry with you for the rest of your life.

Once you get past the sheer size of the University, it will really become a second home. After only a quarter of classes, you won't be able to cross the Oval without seeing someone you know. Ohio State is truly the smallest large university you will find. The people are known for their friendly attitudes, and alumni are scattered across the nation. If you choose to go to OSU, you're choosing a school with a name that's well known, both in the workplace and in the college community. Few students ever regret their time at Ohio State, and most consider their college experience to be among the best offered in the Big Ten and the country.

The Inside Scoop

The Lowdown On...
The Inside Scoop

OSU Slang:

Know the slang, know the school. The following is a list of things you really need to know before coming to OSU. The more of these words you know, the better off you'll be.

Bucknasty – Nickname for the Buckeye Express.

Gold Pants – Award given to football players after they beat Michigan.

McGahee'd – Injuring your knee; named after former Miami Hurricanes running back Willis McGahee.

The Oval – The oval-shaped area in the middle of campus.

TBDBITL – Short for "the Best Damn Band in the Land," a phrase coined by Woody Hayes to describe the Ohio State Marching Band.

That State Up North – The proper way to refer to Michigan.

The 'Schott – Ohio State's arena; the Jerome Schottenstein Center.

The Shoe – Ohio State's football stadium, the Horseshoe.

Woody – Ohio State's most beloved football coach.

Things I Wish I Knew Before Coming to OSU

- You make all your real friends during winter quarter.
- It's not really a big deal if someone you know is gay.
- You're on your own with responsibility—no one makes you do your work.
- You will never use all your meal blocks, no matter how hard you try.
- The workload is intense—five extra hours of work a week per class is about right.
- Not all areas of study receive the same amount of funding.
- Short of going to concerts, there is not much need for a car while living on campus.
- Time management is essential to success.

Tips to Succeed at OSU

- Actually go to class.
- Make friends with classmates and study with them.
- Get to know your teachers and TAs.
- Don't be afraid to read something twice.
- Don't stay undecided for too long.
- If your grade looks too low, ask about it.
- Be open-minded; this isn't high school anymore.

OSU Urban Legends

- There is an underground system of tunnels that connects every building on campus.
- Weigel Hall is haunted.
- A student committed suicide and landed in the Numbers Garden (on the 6).
- ESPN football analyst Trev Alberts couldn't get accepted to OSU, and that's why he hates the football team.

School Spirit

School spirit is an area where Ohio State shines—the school is filled to the brim with spirit. Students have a sort of us-against-the-world mentality, largely due to the fact that outside of Ohio, it's kind of cool to hate OSU. This seems to make students even more proud of being Buckeyes. What other campus sees students jump into a freezing cold lake just to support the football team? Everywhere you go, you can find students decorated in scarlet and gray. Local houses sport the colors as well. Every student knows the words to "Carmen Ohio," and has shed at least one tear while singing it with their closest friends. Buckeyes are fiercely proud of where they come from, and it shows. As the words go: "Time and change will surely show / How firm thy friendship, O-HI-O."

Traditions

School Songs

"Across the Field" and "Buckeye Battle Cry" – Official fight songs

"Carmen Ohio" – Alma mater

"Hang on Sloopy" – Official rock song

"We Don't Give a Damn for the Whole State of Michigan" – Traditional

"Le Regiment" – Traditional march

The Ohio State University Marching Band

The band is where it all begins. Much of the tradition involves football games, so that's what it's mostly focused on. The band is composed of 225 members, all brass and percussion.

Skull Session
Skull Session begins two hours before each home game. The band goes through its upcoming performance in a pep-rally type of atmosphere, while fans pack St. John Arena to listen. Under Coach Jim Tressel, the Buckeye football players now walk through on their way to the locker room before the game.

Ramp
After marching from the Skull Session to the stadium, the band proceeds down a long ramp to take the field. The band forms a large block and bursts into the OSU Fight Song as 100,000 people stand and cheer/sing along.

Script Ohio
In the premier college marching band tradition, the band spells out "Ohio" in large cursive letters on the field. At the very end, the drum major will lead out a fourth-year sousaphone player to dot the letter "i" on the field. Flashbulbs fly and the crowd erupts in applause as the band member performs a salute. Dotting the "i" is a major honor, and it is reserved for marching band members, with few exceptions. Bob Hope and Woody Hayes have dotted the 'i' as well.

Block O
The official student section for football games. Block O sits in the south stands and cheers on the team by holding up signs that show spirit. Past examples include a buckeye leaf, or a drawing of the script Ohio. Block O is highly publicized, and has a storied tradition of cheering on the Buckeyes. It should be noted, however, that the north student section is always louder than Block O, giving the home team a decisive advantage at that end of the stadium.

Other Traditions

When a football game ends, the team gathers on the field in front of the south stands. There, they sing "Carmen Ohio" with the fans while the band plays.

When the football team beats Michigan, the players receive their "Gold Pants"—a gold charm replica of a pair of football pants is given to each of the players.

It is said that if you can walk completely across the Oval, from the Main Library to the seal, while holding your sweetheart's hand, you two will marry each other one day.

If someone yells "O-H!" at you, you must scream "I-O!" back at them. Failure to do so may result in bodily harm.

"Hang on Sloopy" is the official rock song of the state of Ohio. Fans substitute "O-H-I-O" for the lyrics to the chorus. Listen through once, and you'll figure it out.

Fans wear buckeye necklaces to show their spirit.

Finding a Job or Internship

The Lowdown On...
Finding a Job or Internship

If you are worried about locating an internship for the summer or a job after graduation, Ohio State has services to help. The Ohio State Career Services Web site (*www.careers.ohio-state.edu*) can point you in the right direction. The Younkin Success Center is also an option. This office has career counseling and advising available to students on a walk-in or appointment basis. Their programs focus mainly on Internet-based and self-motivated interest exploration, and their Web site offers resources that students can work through on their own time.

The Younkin Success Center
1640 Neil Ave., Room 226
(614) 688-3898
www.careerconnection.osu.edu

Grads Who Enter the Job Market Within
6 Months: 64%
1 Year: N/A

Firms That Most Frequently Hire Grads
Accenture, Bank One, Battelle, and IBM

Alumni

The Lowdown On...
Alumni

Web Site:
www.ohiostatealumni.org

Office:
The Ohio State University Alumni Association Inc.
2200 Olentangy River Road
Columbus, Ohio 43210-1035
(614) 292-2200

Services Available:
Over 123,000 members display their affection towards the University by acting as ambassadors, recruiting outstanding students, and providing financial support for both students and the University. Alumni members also get a free OSU e-mail account.

Visit *www.osu.edu/email* for more information.

Major Alumni Events

Alumni members can purchase football tickets, as well as receive reduced rates on parking. Lots of alumni return for Homecoming in the fall, and they can be seen wandering the campus with their families, pointing out classrooms they attended and residence halls they lived in. Many alumni have special tailgating parties, as well.

Alumni Publications

Alumni Connections is the official magazine of Ohio State Alumni. Published eight times a year, the magazine strives to keep alumni informed of what's going on at Ohio State and what fellow alumni are achieving in the world.

Did You Know?

Famous OSU Alumni:

John Glenn – Astronaut

John Havlicek – Basketball player

Bobby Knight – Basketball coach

Richard Lewis – Actor/comedian

John M. Matthias – Recipient of the Congressional Medal of Honor

Jack Nicklaus – Professional golfer

Jessie Owens – Track & field star

R. L. Stine – Author

James Thurber – Humorist/cartoonist

Dwight Yoakam – Country music artist

Student Organizations

For a complete list of the more than 1,100 student organizations at Ohio State, visit:

www.ohiounion.osu.edu/studentorgs/orgs_directory.asp

All Nations Christian Fellowship
American Cancer Society Colleges Against Cancer
American Society of Interior Designers
Best Buddies International
Business Law Society
Campus Disc Golf Club
Christian Dental Association
College Republicans at The Ohio State University
Columbus Fellowship of Christ
Crops and Soils Club
Dispute Resolution & Youth
Dodgeball Syndicate at OSU
Ecological Engineering Society
Education Against Oppression

Ether

Fellowship of Campus Unitarian Universalists

Film Junkies Anonymous

Fisher College of Business Honors Cohort

Future Songwriters of America

Gay, Lesbian, Bisexual and Transgender Career Paths

Greek Ambassadors

Hillel Student Board of Trustees

Hip Hop at The Ohio State University

Hunger ELimination Project

Institute for Africana Methodologies

Italian Club at Ohio State University

Japanese Club

Jews on Campus

Korean Student Association

Law Students for Immigrant and Refugee Rights at Ohio State

Line Dance Club

MBA Marketing Association

Medieval and Renaissance Performers Guild

Mens Ultimate Disc Club

Nursing Student Council

Objectivist Thinkers at The Ohio State University

Ohio Union Art Board

OSU Entrepreneurs' Association

OSU Fashion Guild

Pathology Interest Club

Queer Christians Student Organization at the Ohio State University

Rifle Club

Ski and Board Club at OSU

The Guitar Player's Club at the Ohio State University

Undergraduate Philosophy Club

The Best & Worst

The Ten BEST Things About Ohio State

1. The Oval on a sunny spring afternoon
2. The Horseshoe on a cold, breezy fall morning
3. Concerts at the Newport
4. The Best Damn Band in the Land competition
5. Michigan Week
6. Brutus Buckeye
7. Huge snowball fights on the Oval
8. Jim Tressel/Woody Hayes (tie)
9. Intramural ice hockey
10. Mirror Lake

The Ten WORST Things About Ohio State

1. Parking
2. Occasional rioting
3. Campus dining
4. Dining at the commons
5. Minimal Greek scene
6. Completely unpredictable weather
7. Hemp Fest
8. The crazy amount of studying needed to succeed
9. RAs on power trips (uncommon, but it happens)
10. Parking

Visiting

The Lowdown On...
Visiting

Hotel Information:

The Blackwell
2110 Tuttle Park Place
(614) 247-4400
www.theblackwell.com
Distance from Campus:
On campus
Price Range: $109–$159

Courtyard Columbus
35 West Spring St.
(614) 228-3200
Distance from Campus:
2.5 miles
Price Range: $89–$124

Cross Country Inn OSU North
3246 Olentangy River Road
(614) 267-4747
Distance from Campus:
2.7 miles
Price Range: $69–$79

Cross Country Inn OSU South
1445 Olentangy River Road
(614) 291-2983
Distance from Campus:
1.5 miles
Price Range: $54–$139

Fairfield Columbus-OSU

3031 Olentangy River Road

(614) 267-1111

Distance from Campus: 2.5 miles

Price Range: $104–$149

Hampton Inn Suites Downtown

501 North High Street

(614) 559-2000

www.hampton-inn.com/hi/columbus-downtown

Distance from Campus: 2 miles

Price Range: $89–$129

Holiday Inn

328 West Lane Ave.

(614) 294-4848

Distance from Campus: Across the street

Price Range: $119–$129

Holiday Inn Express

701 East Hudson St.

(614) 263-7725

Distance from Campus: 2 miles

Price Range: $60–$70

Columbus Marriott North

6500 Doubletree Ave.

(614) 885-1885

www.marriotthotels.com/cmhno

Distance from Campus: 9 miles

Price Range: $109–$125

University Inn

3160 Olentangy River Road

(614) 261-0523

(888) 344-6000 (toll free)

Distance from Campus: 2.6 miles

Price Range: $45–$55

University Plaza Hotel

3110 Olentangy River Road

(614) 267-7461

(877) 677-5292 (toll free)

www.universityplazaosu.com

Distance from Campus: 2.5 miles

Price Range: $111–$125

Take a Campus Virtual Tour

www-afa.adm.ohio-state.edu/undergrad/av/residence_hall_tours.asp

Campus Tours

Ohio State visit requests must be made at least three weeks before the planned visit date. Visits are scheduled for weekdays during the following time periods:

Fall Quarter: September 29–December 5

Winter Quarter: January 12–March 12

Spring Quarter: April 5–June 4

To schedule a visit, check out:
https://campusvisit.osu.edu

Little Sibs Weekend

Each spring, the Parents Association sponsors Sibs Weekend. All students are encouraged to invite younger siblings, family members, or friends to spend the weekend at Ohio State. The event typically takes place during the first weekend of May. The weekend is a chance for younger siblings to experience a part of college life at Ohio State. Residence halls and facilities all across campus put on programs to entertain the visitors. The biggest of these is the West Campus Luau, held annually on the south lawn of the Drake Center. Other events range from Late Night at Larkins to the North Campus Carnival. The list of programming changes from year to year.

For more details, check out the Parents Association online at: *http://parent.osu.edu*

Directions to Campus

Driving from the North
- Take any major highway to I-270.
- Take I-270 to State Route 315 South.
- Exit at Ackerman Road, and turn left.
- Turn right onto High St. Campus begins south of Lane Ave.

Driving from the South
- Take any major highway to I-71 North.
- Take I-71 North to State Route 315 North.
- Exit at Ackerman Road, and turn right.
- Turn right on High Street. Campus begins south of Lane Ave.

Driving from the East
- Take any major highway to I-70 West.
- Take I-70 West to State Route 315 North.
- Exit at Ackerman Rd., and turn right.
- Turn right on High St. Campus begins south of Lane Ave.

Driving from the West
- Take any major highway to I-70 East.
- Take I-70 East to I-670 East to State Route 315 North.
- Exit at Ackerman Rd., and turn right.
- Turn right on High St. Campus begins south of Lane Ave.

From Port Columbus International Airport
- Take I-670 West to State Route 315 North.
- Exit at Ackerman Rd., and turn right.
- Turn right on High St. Campus begins south of Lane Ave.

Words to Know

Academic Probation – A suspension imposed on a student if he or she fails to keep up with the school's minimum academic requirements. Those unable to improve their grades after receiving this warning can face dismissal.

Beer Pong/Beirut – A drinking game involving cups of beer arranged in a pyramid shape on each side of a table. The goal is to get a ping pong ball into one of the opponent's cups by throwing the ball or hitting it with a paddle. If the ball lands in a cup, the opponent is required to drink the beer.

Bid – An invitation from a fraternity or sorority to 'pledge' (join) that specific house.

Blue-Light Phone – Brightly-colored phone posts with a blue light bulb on top. These phones exist for security purposes and are located at various outside locations around most campuses. In an emergency, a student can pick up one of these phones (free of charge) to connect with campus police or a security escort.

Campus Police – Police who are specifically assigned to a given institution. Campus police are typically not regular city officers; they are employed by the university in a full-time capacity.

Club Sports – A level of sports that falls somewhere between varsity and intramural. If a student is unable to commit to a varsity team but has a lot of passion for athletics, a club sport could be a better, less intense option. Even less demanding, intramural (IM) sports often involve no traveling and considerably less time.

Cocaine – An illegal drug. Also known as "coke" or "blow," cocaine often resembles a white crystalline or powdery substance. It is highly addictive and dangerous.

Common Application – An application with which students can apply to multiple schools.

Course Registration – The period of official class selection for the upcoming quarter or semester. Prior to registration, it is best to prepare several back-up courses in case a particular class becomes full. If a course is full, students can place themselves on the waitlist, although this still does not guarantee entry.

Division Athletics – Athletic classifications range from Division I to Division III. Division IA is the most competitive, while Division III is considered to be the least competitive.

Dorm – A dorm (or dormitory) is an on-campus housing facility. Dorms can provide a range of options from suite-style rooms to more communal options that include shared bathrooms. Most first-year students live in dorms. Some upperclassmen who wish to stay on campus also choose this option.

Early Action – An application option with which a student can apply to a school and receive an early acceptance response without a binding commitment. This system is becoming less and less available.

Early Decision – An application option that students should use only if they are certain they plan to attend the school in question. If a student applies using the early decision option and is admitted, he or she is required and bound to attend that university. Admission rates are usually higher among students who apply through early decision, as the student is clearly indicating that the school is his or her first choice.

Ecstasy – An illegal drug. Also known as "E" or "X," ecstasy looks like a pill and most resembles an aspirin. Considered a party drug, ecstasy is very dangerous and can be deadly.

Ethernet – An extremely fast Internet connection available in most university-owned residence halls. To use an Ethernet connection properly, a student will need a network card and cable for his or her computer.

Fake ID – A counterfeit identification card that contains false information. Most commonly, students get fake IDs with altered birthdates so that they appear to be older than 21 (and therefore of legal drinking age). Even though it is illegal, many college students have fake IDs in hopes of purchasing alcohol or getting into bars.

Frosh – Slang for "freshman" or "freshmen."

Hazing – Initiation rituals administered by some fraternities or sororities as part of the pledging process. Many universities have outlawed hazing due to its degrading, and sometimes dangerous, nature.

Intramurals (IMs) – A popular, and usually free, sport league in which students create teams and compete against one another. These sports vary in competitiveness and can include a range of activities—everything from billiards to water polo. IM sports are a great way to meet people with similar interests.

Keg – Officially called a half-barrel, a keg contains roughly 200 12-ounce servings of beer.

LSD – An illegal drug, also known as acid, this hallucinogenic drug most commonly resembles a tab of paper.

Marijuana – An illegal drug, also known as weed or pot; along with alcohol, marijuana is one of the most commonly-found drugs on campuses across the country.

Major –The focal point of a student's college studies; a specific topic that is studied for a degree. Examples of majors include physics, English, history, computer science, economics, business, and music. Many students decide on a specific major before arriving on campus, while others are simply "undecided" until declaring a major. Those who are extremely interested in two areas can also choose to double major.

Meal Block – The equivalent of one meal. Students on a meal plan usually receive a fixed number of meals per week. Each meal, or "block," can be redeemed at the school's dining facilities in place of cash. Often, a student's weekly allotment of meal blocks will be forfeited if not used.

Minor – An additional focal point in a student's education. Often serving as a complement or addition to a student's main area of focus, a minor has fewer requirements and prerequisites to fulfill than a major. Minors are not required for graduation from most schools; however some students who want to explore many different interests choose to pursue both a major and a minor.

Mushrooms – An illegal drug. Also known as "'shrooms," this drug resembles regular mushrooms but is extremely hallucinogenic.

Off-Campus Housing – Housing from a particular landlord or rental group that is not affiliated with the university. Depending on the college, off-campus housing can range from extremely popular to non-existent. Students who choose to live off campus are typically given more freedom, but they also have to deal with possible subletting scenarios, furniture, bills, and other issues. In addition to these factors, rental prices and distance often affect a student's decision to move off campus.

Office Hours – Time that teachers set aside for students who have questions about coursework. Office hours are a good forum for students to go over any problems and to show interest in the subject material.

Pledging – The early phase of joining a fraternity or sorority, pledging takes place after a student has gone through rush and received a bid. Pledging usually lasts between one and two semesters. Once the pledging period is complete and a particular student has done everything that is required to become a member, that student is considered a brother or sister. If a fraternity or a sorority would decide to "haze" a group of students, this initiation would take place during the pledging period.

Private Institution – A school that does not use tax revenue to subsidize education costs. Private schools typically cost more than public schools and are usually smaller.

Prof – Slang for "professor."

Public Institution – A school that uses tax revenue to subsidize education costs. Public schools are often a good value for in-state residents and tend to be larger than most private colleges.

Quarter System (or Trimester System) – A type of academic calendar system. In this setup, students take classes for three academic periods. The first quarter usually starts in late September or early October and concludes right before Christmas. The second quarter usually starts around early to mid–January and finishes up around March or April. The last academic quarter, or "third quarter," usually starts in late March or early April and finishes up in late May or Mid-June. The fourth quarter is summer. The major difference between the quarter system and semester system is that students take more, less comprehensive courses under the quarter calendar.

RA (Resident Assistant) – A student leader who is assigned to a particular floor in a dormitory in order to help to the other students who live there. An RA's duties include ensuring student safety and providing assistance wherever possible.

Recitation – An extension of a specific course; a review session. Some classes, particularly large lectures, are supplemented with mandatory recitation sessions that provide a relatively personal class setting.

Rolling Admissions – A form of admissions. Most commonly found at public institutions, schools with this type of policy continue to accept students throughout the year until their class sizes are met. For example, some schools begin accepting students as early as December and will continue to do so until April or May.

Room and Board – This figure is typically the combined cost of a university-owned room and a meal plan.

Room Draw/Housing Lottery – A common way to pick on-campus room assignments for the following year. If a student decides to remain in university-owned housing, he or she is assigned a unique number that, along with seniority, is used to determine his or her housing for the next year.

Rush – The period in which students can meet the brothers and sisters of a particular chapter and find out if a given fraternity or sorority is right for them. Rushing a fraternity or a sorority is not a requirement at any school. The goal of rush is to give students who are serious about pledging a feel for what to expect.

Semester System – The most common type of academic calendar system at college campuses. This setup typically includes two semesters in a given school year. The fall semester starts around the end of August or early September and concludes before winter vacation. The spring semester usually starts in mid-January and ends in late April or May.

Student Center/Rec Center/Student Union – A common area on campus that often contains study areas, recreation facilities, and eateries. This building is often a good place to meet up with fellow students; depending on the school, the student center can have a huge role or a non-existent role in campus life.

Student ID – A university-issued photo ID that serves as a student's key to school-related functions. Some schools require students to show these cards in order to get into dorms, libraries, cafeterias, and other facilities. In addition to storing meal plan information, in some cases, a student ID can actually work as a debit card and allow students to purchase things from bookstores or local shops.

Suite – A type of dorm room. Unlike dorms that feature communal bathrooms shared by the entire floor, suites offer bathrooms shared only among the suite. Suite-style dorm rooms can house anywhere from two to ten students.

TA (Teacher's Assistant) – An undergraduate or grad student who helps in some manner with a specific course. In some cases, a TA will teach a class, assist a professor, grade assignments, or conduct office hours.

Undergraduate – A student in the process of studying for his or her bachelor's degree.

ABOUT THE CO-AUTHOR

First and foremost, I hope you enjoyed this guidebook, and most importantly, found it somewhat useful in your current search for a college. Now, on to what you really came for—the dirt on me! I'm currently a junior majoring in English here at OSU (duh!), and though I'm leaning towards education, my real passion lies in literature, so yes, I want to be a writer. Currently I have a couple of novels on the back-burner, though I'm not sure they'll see the light of day while I'm in college. Education comes first, kiddos. I was raised in Weslaco, a small town on the southern tip of Texas, and being alone so far away from home while trying to put some much needed wrinkles on my brain has really made me appreciate all those around me. So, while I'm on that thought, I'm going to jump into the cheap family plugs and people whose constant support has helped me along the way.

Now, I wouldn't be a good son if I didn't thank the two people who decided it was a good idea to bring another person into this world—Mom, Dad, without you nothing would be possible. Thank you to Rose, Danny, Laura, Robert, Grandma, Steve, Ame, Dillon, Bob, Erin, all of my extended family, the lovely Christina for having patience with me, Luke for giving me the opportunity, and of course, everyone else at College Prowler!

Roland Becerra
rolandbecerra@collegeprowler.com

ABOUT THE CO-AUTHOR

Before I say anything about myself, I have to thank the people that made this possible. First, thanks to God and Jesus Christ, through whom all things are possible. An incredible amount of thanks also goes to my family: Mom, Dad, Amy, Andy, and Rodney, who have always supported me in everything I have decided to do. I developed my love of writing in the Northwood School District, so I have to thank Mrs. Karrick, Mrs. James, and of course, Mr. Laird for all seeing some talent in me and nurturing that (until I started writing for *Power of the Pen* in eighth grade, I hated English!). Special shout outs to my friends, both at home in Northwood and the Bucknutty ones here at OSU. Thanks to Oasis, the Beatles, Travis, Blink-182, and Ben Folds, whose music played incessantly while I worked on this project. And of course, thanks to College Prowler for giving me this opportunity.

As for me, I am currently a senior honors student here at "the" Ohio State University (don't ever forget the "the!") majoring in journalism. I have been the sports editor and the opinions editor of the *Lantern*, and I am now the editor-in-chief. I am also the music editor for the *Sentinel* and an arena reporter for the United States College Hockey Organizations Web site (*www.uscho.com*). If all goes well, this will not be the last time you see my name on a book. I am a 2001 graduate of Northwood High school, and I was salutatorian of my class. Upon graduation, I hope to continue writing for a magazine of some sort (*Rolling Stone*, *Sports Illustrated*, *Spin*, are you listening?). I am thankful for all the good times I have had while being a Buckeye, and I look forward to all the benefits that come with it. Carmen Ohio sums it up best: "Time and change will surely show/How firm thy friendship O-HI-O!"

Adam Jardy
adamjardy@collegeprowler.com

California Colleges

California dreamin'?
This book is a must have for you!

CALIFORNIA COLLEGES
7¼" X 10", 762 Pages Paperback
$29.95 Retail
1-59658-501-3

Stanford, UC Berkeley, Caltech—California is home to some of America's greatest institutes of higher learning. *California Colleges* gives the lowdown on 24 of the best, side by side, in one prodigious volume.

New England Colleges

**Looking for peace in the Northeast?
Pick up this regional guide to New England!**

NEW ENGLAND COLLEGES
7¼" X 10", 1015 Pages Paperback
$29.95 Retail
1-59658-504-8

New England is the birthplace of many prestigious universities, and with so many to choose from, picking the right school can be a tough decision. With inside information on over 34 competitive Northeastern schools, *New England Colleges* provides the same high-quality information prospective students expect from College Prowler in one all-inclusive, easy-to-use reference.

Schools of the South

Headin' down south? This book will help you find your way to the perfect school!

SCHOOLS OF THE SOUTH
7¼" X 10", 773 Pages Paperback
$29.95 Retail
1-59658-503-X

Southern pride is always strong. Whether it's across town or across state, many Southern students are devoted to their home sweet home. *Schools of the South* offers an honest student perspective on 36 universities available south of the Mason-Dixon.

Untangling the Ivy League

The ultimate book for everything Ivy!

UNTANGLING THE IVY LEAGUE
7¼" X 10", 567 Pages Paperback
$24.95 Retail
1-59658-500-5

Ivy League students, alumni, admissions officers, and other top insiders get together to tell it like it is. *Untangling the Ivy League* covers every aspect—from admissions and athletics to secret societies and urban legends—of the nation's eight oldest, wealthiest, and most competitive colleges and universities.

Need Help Paying For School?
Apply for our scholarship!

College Prowler awards thousands of dollars a year to students who compose the best essays. E-mail scholarship@collegeprowler.com for more information, or call 1-800-290-2682.

Apply now at **www.collegeprowler.com**

COLLEGE PROWLER®

Tell Us What Life Is Really Like at Your School!

Have you ever wanted to let people know what your college is really like? Now's your chance to help millions of high school students choose the right college.

Let your voice be heard.

Check out ***www.collegeprowler.com*** for more info!

COLLEGE PROWLER®

Need More Help?

Do you have more questions about this school? Can't find a certain statistic? College Prowler is here to help. We are the best source of college information out there. We have a network of thousands of students who can get the latest information on any school to you ASAP. E-mail us at info@collegeprowler.com with your college-related questions.

E-Mail Us Your College-Related Questions!

Check out *www.collegeprowler.com* for more details.
1-800-290-2682

COLLEGE PROWLER®

Write For Us!
Get published! Voice your opinion.

Writing a College Prowler guidebook is both fun and rewarding; our open-ended format allows your own creativity free reign. Our writers have been featured in national newspapers and have seen their names in bookstores across the country. Now is your chance to break into the publishing industry with one of the country's fastest-growing publishers!

Apply now at **www.collegeprowler.com**

Contact editor@collegeprowler.com or
call 1-800-290-2682 for more details.

COLLEGE PROWLER®

Pros and Cons

Still can't figure out if this is the right school for you? You've already read through this in-depth guide; why not list the pros and cons? It will really help with narrowing down your decision and determining whether or not this school is right for you.

Pros	Cons
....	....
....	....
....	....
....	....
....	....
....	....
....	....
....	....
....	....
....	....
....	....
....	....
....	....
....	....

COLLEGE PROWLER®

Pros and Cons

Still can't figure out if this is the right school for you? You've already read through this in-depth guide; why not list the pros and cons? It will really help with narrowing down your decision and determining whether or not this school is right for you.

Pros	Cons
....	....
....	....
....	....
....	....
....	....
....	....
....	....
....	....
....	....
....	....
....	....
....	....
....	....
....	....

COLLEGE PROWLER®

Notes

Notes

Notes

Notes

Notes

Notes

Notes

Notes

Notes

Notes

Notes

Notes

Notes

Notes

Notes

Notes

Notes

Notes

Notes

Notes

Notes

Notes

Notes

Notes

Notes

Notes

Notes